The City Of Dreadful Night

Series Editor:
Anne McManus Scriven

The
City of Dreadful Night

and Other Poems

James Thomson

with an introduction by
Ian Campbell

Kennedy & Boyd
an imprint of
Zeticula
57 St Vincent Crescent
Glasgow
G3 8NQ
Scotland

http://www.kennedyandboyd.co.uk
admin@kennedyandboyd.co.uk

First published in 1874
This edition Copyright © Kennedy & Boyd 2008
Introduction Copyright © Kennedy & Boyd 2008

Cover photograph Copyright © Hamid Masoumi 2008

ISBN-13 978 1 904999 72 0
ISBN-10   1 904999 72 7

Contents

Introduction.

The facts of James Thomson's short and unhappy life are
familiar and quickly told. Born in Port Glasgow in 1834,
he early lost his parents, was raised in an orphanage and
received his scanty education in the Royal Military Academy
in Woolwich. He served in the Army, worked briefly in the
USA, held a succession of clerical jobs and all the time wrote.
His poetry and prose and essays all show a well-stocked and
wide-ranging intelligence, allied to a deeply felt alienation
which was encouraged by his contact with the secularist
movement of his time, especially Charles Bradlaugh and
through him the *National Reformer*, where he published a
good deal. Unhappy in love, he became progressively weaker
as alcohol and insomnia took their toll, and though he had
many friends and was capable of friendship in a loyal circle,
he retreated more and more into melancholy before dying
in 1882 at the age of 47. Thomson's fame rests largely on
The City of Dreadful Night, written 1870-74, though his
other work repays study and shows the influence of his
wide reading, above all in Italian literature: he was to be an
important influence on the following century's poets above all
T.S.Eliot, and he had a powerful admirer in Edwin Morgan
whose introduction to the Canongate edition of *The City*
remains the best brief cogent critical discussion.

*

The City of Dreadful Night is a long and challenging
poem. Its 21 sections describe an imagined journey through
darkness, doubt and finally despair which resonates with the
felt experience of a man who battled loneliness, sleeplessness
and the ravages of alcohol, and sought to communicate to
an age not quite ready to find expression for the idea of the
impossibility of a Christian God and a Christian world. While

writers like George Eliot found ways of communicating this radical and potentially explosive conviction in works of fiction, Thomson in *The City of Dreadful Night* set out to depict such a world in terms so vivid that the reader would be drawn into accepting the reality of its premise – a Godless Universe, a godless society, an all-encompassing darkness which leads not to apocalypse but to a deadening despair – the poem's last words, in fact. If Eliot was to write in *The Hollow Men* (1925) of the world's end "not with a bang but a whimper",[1] if Wells was to imagine the world's end in a lonely desolate beach as the Earth, lifeless, runs out of energy and faces a cold, dark eclipse in *The Time Machine* (1895), Thomson had earlier envisioned such an anti-apocalypse to challenge the Bible's vision of noise, energy, blinding light, glorious eternity and fiery judgement. *The City of Dreadful Night* is constructed round silence, the absence of energy, all-encompassing darkness, terrifying timelessness and the utter absence of the certainties which underlie any idea of judgement – the "real night" of section 12.

How the poem is structured is important, for so intense is its focus on this central vision of emptiness and hopelessness, that it would be easy for the reader to tire after a few sections. The basic method is that of the journey, obviously drawn in inspiration from Dante (and finding an echo in Eliot's *Waste Land* several decades later). Dante, or Bunyan's Christian, would make the journey into unknown territory seeking certainty or faith or some resolution of their doubt: Thomson's wanderer in the poem does not really know why he is making the journey, and he does not learn from it so much as experience it against a matt background of dull acceptance, "weary on a pillar's base",[2] the central intelligence of the poem "sunk in stupor, that dull swoon / which drugs and with a leaden mantle drapes / The outworn to worse weariness".[3] Bunyan's pilgrim is charged with ambition:

Thomson's lacks it at the outset, and his "worse weariness"[4] is the outcome of the succession of experiences the poem confronts him with. This is never more obvious than in the poem's most powerful section, 4, and the vision of the woman with the red lamp in her hand. The poem offers false hope, this early, that the journey has reached some conclusion, that the empty wandering has led to an acceptance – a figure so obviously related to Mary the mother of Jesus, to the archetypal mother, to the Christian image of the bleeding heart of compassion. Yet section 4 achingly, denies this hope by having the narrative voice trap itself in a false "me" while the other "me" is swept into the mother's arms and the sea carries them both off. The Biblical echoes are more than obvious — Mary with the body of the dead Christ (*John* 20), the *Pieta* of renaissance sculpture, the woman who washed Christ's feet (*Luke* 7), the woman taken in adultery (*John* 8) — but any expectation that we are offered some release from the trap of mortality and loneliness is cruelly contradicted by the paralysed narrator witnessing "that senseless me" being carried away, "and they were borne / Away, and this vile me was left forlorn".[5] Is there an echo of creation and life coming from the sea? Of the rumblings of evolutionary debate which convulsed the intellectuals of Thomson's time? Whatever the effect on the reader's imagination, the result is to offer a possibility of redemption and love, then to deny it with the narrator's bewildered awakening – "But I, what do I here?"[6] – an unanswered question which resonates through the whole poem.

What section 4, and the picture of the woman with the lamp (a cruel parody, perhaps, of Florence Nightingale and the Crimea?) achieves, is an astonishing reversal of reader expectation, and in microcosm it helps explain some of the power of *The City of Dreadful Night*. To the reader of the 1870s, the city represented an immense social organism, and in the hands of a Dickens or a Thackeray it pulsed with enormous diversity of life. In the literal sense, it increasingly incorporated the emerging technologies of rail and steam, and as the cities grew in size they became bewildering, threatening, but always instinct with life and possibility. Not so this city; the journey through the city is from one false start to another, from one encounter which may explain or give hope to another, but not to destination or to core of meaning or final explanation. Thomson designs the poem as a series of small journeys, each one anticlimactically leading to another false start, and the conclusion (section 20) is a masterpiece of denial of the reader's expectation – a final confrontation, good and evil, light and darkness – what *Revelation* memorably imagines in Scripture – which in Thomson's hands becomes a paralysed vision of failure, enigma, entropy. While the angelic form may have collapsed of its own volition, "shattered" like Ozymandias' futile dreams of victory and eternal power in Shelley's poem, the "sphinx supreme" has not even moved – "changeless as life's laws",[7] it has no need to fight, for life's laws are those of "infinite void space",[8] and the poem's journey is to nowhere, not to realisation or to climax. The imagery of the very last section, 21, reinforces these points: the book is clasped, the eyes sightless, the scientific instruments lying scattered, the wings powerless, but "sustained by indomitable will"[9] to continue to live in a world not understood, where "Fate holds no prize to crown success".[10] Like Pope in the climax of the *Dunciad*, Thomson ends the poem with heroic darkness rather than with energy: but where Pope mockingly described a literary London sunk into ignorance and stupidity, Thomson in all seriousness is describing a philosophy of "the vast black veil uncertain / Because there is no light beyond the curtain",[11] the antithesis of Tennyson's tentative hope in *In Memoriam* that there might be something better "behind the veil". For Tennyson it is one possibility: "O life as futile,

x

then, as frail! / O for thy voice to soothe and bless! / What hope of answer, or redress? / Behind the veil, behind the veil."[12] With this possibility Tennyson offered his readers some hope to set against the Darwinian nightmare, upsetting the long-held views of those "Who trusted God was love indeed / And love Creation's final law - / Tho' Nature, red in tooth and claw / With ravine, shriek'd against his creed-".[13] Not so Thomson: for his stronger readers he offers only "iron endurance", for the weaker, "new terrors".[14] The very last lines of *The City of Dreadful Night* are worth pausing on – for here we have a confirmed post-Christian poet appealing not to a new vision of godlessness, but to "confirmation of the old despair".[15] The *old* despair? If we look at the poem's opening, the "proem" assumes already that people have passed beyond "false dreams, false hopes, false masks and modes of youth",[16] and in an easily overlooked passage Thomson stakes out his territory for *The City of Dreadful Night*:

> For none of these I write, and none of these
>   Could read the writing if they deigned to try:
>   […]
> Nay, be assured; no secret can be told
>   To any who divined it not before:
> None uninitiate by many a presage
> Will comprehend the language of the message,
>   Although proclaimed aloud for evermore.[17]

The poem makes this radical assumption: it is not swimming alone against the tide of Victorian opinion, but appealing to a body of readers who already feel, perhaps believe, the poem's basic premise, but either lack the means of expression, or are unwilling to give voice to a set of beliefs inimical to what was still, to many Victorians, the public consensus of belief.

*

Given that this is potentially explosive territory, how does the poem use Thomson's undoubted talents as a writer to capture the reader's imagination and, possibly, assent? To say the poem is uneven is hardly to exaggerate, for while the journey *motif* allows for alternation and fresh starts, the vividness with which the city is depicted varies very much. There are several evident techniques. One is the carrying through the poem of predominant imagery: darkness, established at the outset, is still the overwhelming feature at the end. Given the oft-repeated use of imagery of light and sunshine in religious writing, and in Scripture, this *motif* offers a strong and unifying stimulus to the reader's imagination. In the 1870s, artificial illumination was becoming more and more accessible to Victorian society in the form of gaslight: Dickens in his novels (one thinks of the Fairy Palaces in *Hard Times*) repeatedly contrasts the darkness of the city with the light of workplace, office or affluent home. Few places would have illustrated this more vividly to the Victorian than the well-filled and well-lit church buildings, and Thomson vividly appeals to this in section 14 with his picture of the church at the city's heart, the superb figure of the charismatic preacher, and his unforgettable text "O melancholy Brothers, dark, dark, dark!"[18] Thomson's mother had been an adherent of Edward Irving's Catholic Apostolic church, and he will have been familiar with descriptions of Irving — whose appearance and preaching style are uncannily caught in this section, as any reader of Irving's life (or Carlyle's *Reminiscences*) would recognize. Tall, with jet-black hair, dark clothes and a splendid voice, Irving held his congregations for hours as he sermonized: this scene parodies such a sermon with its reversal of expectation and text.

And now at last authentic word I bring,
Witnessed by every dead and living thing;
   Good tidings of great joy for you, for all;

There is no God; no Fiend with names divine
Made us and tortures us; if we must pine,
   It is to satiate no Being's gall.[19]

Few readers of the time would have missed the ironic
reversal – the "good tidings of great joy" brought by the
angel at Christ's birth illuminated by the star in the East
(*Luke* 2) – but Thomson manages to make the astonishing
bald statement "There is no God" fit into the texture of the
section without offence, partly by putting into the mouth of
the preacher rather than the ostensible words of the poet,
partly by putting such a text into a context of such reversed
values. For the four words do indeed contradict so many
readers' assumptions that they have to be implanted in a dense
texture: in few places is this more successfully done, apart
from this anti-sermon, than in the reversal of the walk in
the wilderness in Scripture where Moses found illumination
(*Exodus*), or Jesus resisted temptation (*Matthew* 4, *Mark* 1,
Luke 4). Section 4 is very self-aware in its reversal of Biblical
text – the reference to the burning bush is obvious (*Exodus*
3) – and the voice of the wanderer through the wilderness
is looking for illumination, and finds rather one of the most
extraordinary of Thomson's effective uses of darkness.

As I came through the desert thus is was,
As I came through the desert: On the left
The sun arose and crowned a broad crag-cleft;
There stopped and burned out black, except a rim,
A bleeding eyeless socket, red and dim;
Whereon the moon fell suddenly south-west,
And stood above the right-hand cliffs at rest:
    Yet I strode on austere;
    No hope could have no fear.[20]

The bringing together of a number of striking images in one highly-pressured part of the poem is characteristic of Thomson's technique at its best: these nine lines combine an unnatural conjunction of sun and moon, a total eclipse (one of the rarest and most striking disturbances of nature), and one of literature's most grotesque and unpleasant metaphors, perfectly capturing the appearance of total eclipse, yet simultaneously repelling the reader with the nightmare imagining of an eyeless socket – or the fear of blindness, surely one of the most primitive fears of any reader. Whether or not the reader catches the reference to Gloucester's blindness in *Lear* – who never saw till he lost his eyes – the envisioning of the idea that – baldly – "There is no God" - could hardly be better achieved than through this striking conjunction of the unnatural phenomenon and the unnatural darkness which comes with it. Only in the darkness of the post-God world, Thomson's imagery presses us to imagine, can we really see the truth. The idea is as horrible as the wilderness he tramps through en route to this vision (with monsters whose "clanking wings" unpleasantly suggest a threatening machine universe, as well as a post-Darwinian dystopia) and as comfortless as the light the mysterious woman carries in her hand – which turns out, also in repellent physical detail, to be her own heart. The attack on the religious iconography of the sacred heart is no doubt intentional on Thomson's part: if *The City of Dreadful Night* is to have its effect, it has to break through the layers with which readers protect themselves both from unpleasant physical imagining, and revolutionary and upsetting ideas.

Imagery is at the heart of this scene, and throughout at the root of Thomson's success when he carries the reader from one journey to the next towards the dead heart of the city. To be sure, the effect can be overdone, when Thomson's ear betrays him to excess – "White foambelts seethed there, wan spray swept and flew",[21] or

A Sabbath of the Serpents, heaped pell-mell
For Devil's roll-call and some *fête* of Hell [22]

There can be too much assonance and alliteration, however
effective it can be at times –

> A woman very young and very fair;
> Beloved by bounteous life and joy and youth,
> And loving these sweet lovers, so that care
> And age and death seemed not for her in sooth [23]

and Thomson can sometimes not resist the capping of a
successful line by another

> Infections of unutterable sadness,
> Infections of incalculable madness,
> Infections of incurable despair. [24]

The poem's power is undeniable when read aloud: the
stanza form, unfortunately, can lead to predictable rhymes
and a sense that the point has been made too often. The
success comes, as has been suggested, from the predominant
conceit of the *journey* where expectation of destination or
enlightenment is disappointed, and the predominant imagery
of *darkness* which underlines the snuffing out of religious
faith, so often expressed in Scripture and in Christian writing
in terms of light and the sun.

*

It is easy to read into *The City of Dreadful Night* the
loneliness and despair that Thomson must himself have
experienced as he lost love, career, money and health and fell
more and more into depression, insomnia (a theme expressed
terribly vividly in some of his other poetry) and despair. His
life was driven by the need to write, to make money, by a

sense of apartness as he wrote against what still seemed the public current of his age. The success of the poem can best be judged by repeated reading, to appreciate the repetitive effects, the architecture of effect caused by repetition of motif and image, the denial of imagery from the Bible, the denial of imagery of a journey towards fulfillment or enlightenment, the denial of reader expectation that the journey will lead to confrontation, to order, to victory, anything but this sense of trapped helplessness which Thomson expresses from the "proem" onwards. The confrontation of angel with sphinx is masterly: tradition prepares the reader for the pinning of the dragon to the ground by the angel, but the poem does not even reverse this outcome – it simply passes it by. "Confirmation of the old despair" follows on to those "initiate by many a presage"[25] who had reached this territory even before they opened the poem. And to those who had not yet made this journey, Thomson's poem offers a vivid and often terrifying glimpse of a world which the next century was to explore in many hearts of darkness.

Further Reading.

Edwin Morgan's brief but excellent introduction to the Canongate edition of the poem (Canongate Classics, 53: Edinburgh, 1993) remains the best starting point, and gives reference to other valuable recent work, such as Robert Crawford, *The Savage and the City*, Oxford, 1987). Anne Ridler has a good, but scarce, one-volume anthology of Thomson in the Centaur Press (London, 1963), and W.D. Schaefer has both edited a selection of Thomson's prose (*The Speedy Extinction of Evil and Misery*, Berkeley and Los Angeles, 1967) and written a lucid introduction (*Beyond the City*, Berkeley and Los Angeles, 1965). Tom Leonard's *Places of the Mind: The Life and Work of James Thomson* (London, 1993) is incisive and very helpful in reading the poem. There is a splendid brief passage on the poem in David Daiches' *God and the Poets* (Oxford, 1984). A discussion which incorporates some of Thomson's other work is "'And I Burn Too': Thomson's City of Dreadful Night", *Victorian Poetry* 16, 1/2 (Spring/ Summer 1978), 123-33. Reprinted in *Nineteenth-Century Literature Criticism* ed. Janet Mullane (Detroit,1988).

Ian Campbell.

1.   Eliot, T.S. (1925) 'The Hollow Men', (rpt., 1974) *Collected Poems 1909-1962*. London: Faber. p.92
2.   Thomson, James, (1874 rpt., 2008) *The City of Dreadful Night and Other Poems*. Glasgow: Kennedy and Boyd. Section 20, line 1, p.38
3.   *Ibid.*, section 20, line 1, lines 20-22, p.39
4.   *Ibid.*, section 4, lines 100-101, p.13
5.   *Ibid.*, section 4, line 106, p.13
6.   *Ibid.*, section 20, line 42, p.39
7.   *Ibid.*, section 20, line 48, p.40
8.   *Ibid.*, section 21, line 52, p.42
9.   *Ibid.*, section 21, line 65, p.42
10.   *Ibid.*, section 21, line 68-69, p.42
11.   Tennyson, Alfred, (1849) *In Memoriam*. Section LVI. (rpt., 1991) Day, A,(ed.) *Alfred Tennyson: Selected Poems*. London: Penguin. pp.165-6.
12.   *Ibid.*,
13.   Thomson, J, (1874 rpt., 2008), Section 21, line 82-83, p. 43
14.   *Ibid.*, Section 21, line 84
15.   *Ibid.*, 'Proem', line 10, p.3
16.   *Ibid.*, lines 22-24, pp.3-4
17.   *Ibid.*, Section 14, line 25, p.28
18.   *Ibid.*, Section 14, lines 37-42, p29
19.   *Ibid.*, Section 4, lines 52-60, p.12
20.   *Ibid.*, Section 4, line 48, p.11
21.   *Ibid.*, Section 4, lines 30-31, p.11
22.   *Ibid.*, Section 10, lines 25-28, p.21
23.   *Ibid.*, Section 15, lines 19-21. p.31
24.   *Ibid.*, 'Proem', line 40, p.4

The City of Dreadful Night

Per me si va nella città dolente.

DANTE.

Poi di tanto adoprar, di tanti moti
D'ogni celeste, ogni terrena cosa,
Girando senza posa,
Per tornar sempre là donde son mosse;
Uso alcuno, alcun frutto
Indovinar non so.

Sola nel mondo eterna, a cui si volve
Ogni creata cosa,
In te, morte, si posa
Nostra ignuda natura;
Lieta no, ma sicura
Dell'antico dolor . . .
Però ch' esser beato
Nega ai mortali e nega a' morti il fato.

LEOPARDI.

Proem.

Lo, thus, as prostrate, 'In the dust I write
  My heart's deep languor and my soul's sad tears.'
Yet why evoke the spectres of black night
  To blot the sunshine of exultant years?
Why disinter dead faith from mouldering hidden?
Why break the seals of mute despair unbidden,
  And wail life's discords into careless ears?

Because a cold rage seizes one at whiles
  To show the bitter old and wrinkled truth
Stripped naked of all vesture that beguiles,
  False dreams, false hopes, false masks and modes of youth;
Because it gives some sense of power and passion
In helpless impotence to try to fashion
  Our woe in living words howe'er uncouth.

Surely I write not for the hopeful young,
  Or those who deem their happiness of worth,
Or such as pasture and grow fat among
  The shows of life and feel nor doubt nor dearth,
Or pious spirits with a God above them
To sanctify and glorify and love them,
  Or sages who foresee a heaven on earth.

For none of these I write, and none of these
  Could read the writing if they deigned to try:
So may they flourish, in their due degrees,
  On our sweet earth and in their unplaced sky.
If any cares for the weak words here written,
It must be some one desolate, Fate-smitten,
  Whose faith and hope are dead, and who would die.

Yes, here and there some weary wanderer
   In that same city of tremendous night,
Will understand the speech, and feel a stir
   Of fellowship in all-disastrous fight;
'I suffer mute and lonely, yet another
Uplifts his voice to let me know a brother
   Travels the same wild paths though out of sight.'

O sad Fraternity, do I unfold
   Your dolorous mysteries shrouded from of yore?
Nay, be assured; no secret can be told
   To any who divined it not before:
None uninitiate by many a presage
Will comprehend the language of the message,
   Although proclaimed aloud for evermore.

I

The City is of Night; perchance of Death,
   But certainly of Night; for never there
Can come the lucid morning's fragrant breath
   After the dewy dawning's cold grey air;
The moon and stars may shine with scorn or pity;
The sun has never visited that city,
   For it dissolveth in the daylight fair.

Dissolveth like a dream of night away;
   Though present in distempered gloom of thought
And deadly weariness of heart all day.
   But when a dream night after night is brought
Throughout a week, and such weeks few or many
Recur each year for several years, can any
   Discern that dream from real life in aught?

For life is but a dream whose shapes return,
  Some frequently, some seldom, some by night
And some by day, some night and day: we learn,
  The while all change and many vanish quite,
In their recurrence with recurrent changes
A certain seeming order; where this ranges
  We count things real; such is memory's might.

A river girds the city west and south,
  The main north channel of a broad lagoon,
Regurging with the salt tides from the mouth;
  Waste marshes shine and glister to the moon
For leagues, then moorland black, then stony ridges;
Great piers and causeways, many noble bridges,
  Connect the town and islet suburbs strewn.

Upon an easy slope it lies at large,
  And scarcely overlaps the long curved crest
Which swells out two leagues, from the river marge.
  A trackless wilderness rolls north and west,
Savannahs, savage woods, enormous mountains,
Bleak uplands, black ravines with torrent fountains;
  And eastward rolls the shipless sea's unrest.

The city is not ruinous, although
  Great ruins of an unremembered past,
With others of a few short years ago
  More sad, are found within its precincts vast.
The street-lamps always burn; but scarce a casement
In house or palace front from roof to basement
  Doth glow or gleam athwart the mirk air cast.

The street-lamps burn amidst the baleful glooms,
  Amidst the soundless solitudes immense
Of rangèd mansions dark and still as tombs.
  The silence which benumbs or strains the sense
Fulfils with awe the soul's despair unweeping:
Myriads of habitants are ever sleeping,
  Or dead, or fled from nameless pestilence!

Yet as in some necropolis you find
  Perchance one mourner to a thousand dead,
So there; worn faces that look deaf and blind
  Like tragic masks of stone. With weary tread,
Each wrapt in his own doom, they wander, wander,
Or sit foredone and desolately ponder
  Through sleepless hours with heavy drooping head.

Mature men chiefly, few in age or youth,
  A woman rarely, now and then a child:
A child! If here the heart turns sick with ruth
  To see a little one from birth defiled,
Or lame or blind, as preordained to languish
Through youthless life, think how it bleeds with anguish
  To meet one erring in that homeless wild.

They often murmur to themselves, they speak
  To one another seldom, for their woe
Broods maddening inwardly and scorns to wreak
  Itself abroad; and if at whiles it grow
To frenzy which must rave, none heeds the clamour,
Unless there waits some victim of like glamour,
  To rave in turn, who lends attentive show.

The City is of Night, but not of Sleep;
　There sweet sleep is not for the weary brain;
The pitiless hours like years and ages creep,
　A night seems termless hell. This dreadful strain
Of thought and consciousness which never ceases,
Or which some moments' stupor but increases,
　This, worse than woe, makes wretches there insane.

They leave all hope behind who enter there:
　One certitude while sane they cannot leave,
One anodyne for torture and despair;
　The certitude of Death, which no reprieve
Can put off long; and which, divinely tender,
But waits the outstretched hand to promptly render
　That draught whose slumber nothing can bereave.*

* Though the Garden of thy Life be wholly waste, the sweet flowers withered, the fruit-trees
barren, over its wall hang ever the rich dark clusters of the Vine of Death, within easy reach
of thy hand, which may pluck of them when it will.

II

Because he seemed to walk with an intent
　I followed him; who shadowlike and frail,
Unswervingly though slowly onward went,
　Regardless, wrapt in thought as in a veil:
Thus step for step with lonely sounding feet
We travelled many a long dim silent street.

At length he paused: a black mass in the gloom,
　A tower that merged into the heavy sky;
Around, the huddled stones of grave and tomb:
　Some old God's-acre now corruption's sty:
He murmured to himself with dull despair,

Here Faith died, poisoned by this charnel air.
Then turning to the right went on once more,
  And travelled weary roads without suspense;
And reached at last a low wall's open door,
  Whose villa gleamed beyond the foliage dense:
He gazed, and muttered with a hard despair,
Here Love died, stabbed by its own worshipped pair.

Then turning to the right resumed his march,
  And travelled streets and lanes with wondrous strength,
Until on stooping through a narrow arch
  We stood before a squalid house at length:
He gazed, and whispered with a cold despair,
Here Hope died, starved out in its utmost lair.

When he had spoken thus, before he stirred,
  I spoke, perplexed by something in the signs
Of desolation I had seen and heard
  In this drear pilgrimage to ruined shrines:
When Faith and Love and Hope are dead indeed,
Can Life still live? By what doth it proceed?

As whom his one intense thought overpowers,
  He answered coldly, Take a watch, erase
The signs and figures of the circling hours,
  Detach the hands, remove the dial-face;
The works proceed until run down; although
Bereft of purpose, void of use, still go.

Then turning to the right paced on again,
  And traversed squares and travelled streets whose glooms
Seemed more and more familiar to my ken;
  And reached that sullen temple of the tombs;
And paused to murmur with the old despair,

Here Faith died, poisoned by this charnel air.
I ceased to follow, for the knot of doubt
  Was severed sharply with a cruel knife:
He circled thus for ever tracing out
  The series of the fraction left of Life;
Perpetual recurrence in the scope
Of but three terms, dead Faith, dead Love, dead Hope.*

* Life divided by that persistent three <u>LXX</u>   . .
$$\overline{333} = .210.$$

III

Although lamps burn along the silent streets;
  Even when moonlight silvers empty squares
The dark holds countless lanes and close retreats;
  But when the night its sphereless mantle wears
The open spaces yawn with gloom abysmal,
The sombre mansions loom immense and dismal,
  The lanes are black as subterranean lairs.

And soon the eye a strange new vision learns:
  The night remains for it as dark and dense,
Yet clearly in this darkness it discerns
  As in the daylight with its natural sense;
Perceives a shade in shadow not obscurely,
Pursues a stir of black in blackness surely,
  Sees spectres also in the gloom intense.

The ear, too, with the silence vast and deep
  Becomes familiar though unreconciled;
Hears breathings as of hidden life asleep,
  And muffled throbs as of pent passions wild,
Far murmurs, speech of pity or derision;

But all more dubious than the things of vision,
  So that it knows not when it is beguiled.
No time abates the first despair and awe,
  But wonder ceases soon; the weirdest thing
Is felt least strange beneath the lawless law
  Where Death-in-Life is the eternal king;
Crushed impotent beneath this reign of terror,
Dazed with such mysteries of woe and error,
  The soul is too outworn for wondering.

IV

He stood alone within the spacious square
  Declaiming from the central grassy mound,
With head uncovered and with streaming hair,
  As if large multitudes were gathered round:
A stalwart shape, the gestures full of might,
The glances burning with unnatural light: —

As I came through the desert thus it was,
As I came through the desert: All was black
In heaven no single star, on earth no track;
A brooding hush without a stir or note,
The air so thick it clotted in my throat;
And thus for hours; then some enormous things
Swooped past with savage cries and clanking wings
  But I strode on austere;
  No hope could have no fear.

As I came through the desert thus it was,
As I came through the desert: Eyes of fire
Glared at me throbbing with a starved desire;
The hoarse and heavy and carnivorous breath

Was hot upon me from deep jaws of death;
Sharp claws, swift talons, fleshless fingers cold
Plucked at me from the bushes, tried to hold:
  But I strode on austere;
  No hope could have no fear.

As I came through the desert thus it was,
As I came through the desert: Lo you, there,
That hillock burning with a brazen glare;
Those myriad dusky flames with points a-glow
Which writhed and hissed and darted to and fro;
A Sabbath of the Serpents, heaped pell-mell
For Devil's roll-call and some *fête* of Hell:
  Yet I strode on austere;
  No hope could have no fear.

As I came through the desert thus it was,
As I came through the desert: Meteors ran
And crossed their javelins on the black sky-span;
The zenith opened to a gulf of flame,
The dreadful thunderbolts jarred earth's fixed frame:
The ground all heaved in waves of fire that surged
And weltered round me sole there unsubmerged:
  Yet I strode on austere;
  No hope could have no fear.

As I came through the desert thus it was,
As I came through the desert: Air once more,
And I was close upon a wild sea-shore;
Enormous cliffs arose on either hand,
The deep tide thundered up a league-broad strand;
White foambelts seethed there, wan spray swept and flew;
The sky broke, moon and stars and clouds and blue:
  And I rode on austere;
  No hope could have no fear.

As I came through the desert thus it was,
As I came through the desert: On the left
The sun arose and crowned a broad crag-cleft;
There stopped and burned out black, except a rim,
A bleeding eyeless socket, red and dim;
Whereon the moon fell suddenly south-west,
And stood above the right-hand cliffs at rest:
  Still I strode on austere;
  No hope could have no fear.

As I came through the desert thus it was,
As I came through the desert: From the right
A shape came slowly with a ruddy light;
A woman with a red lamp in her hand,
Bareheaded and barefooted on that strand;
O desolation moving with such grace!
O anguish with such beauty in thy face!
  I fell as on my bier,
  Hope travailed with such fear.

As I came through the desert thus it was,
As I came through the desert: I was twain,
Two selves distinct that cannot join again;
One stood apart and knew but could not stir,
And watched the other stark in swoon and her;
And she came on, and never turned aside,
Between such sun and moon and roaring tide:
  And as she came more near
  My soul grew mad with fear.

As I came through the desert thus it was,
As I came through the desert: Hell is mild
And piteous matched with that accursèd wild;
A large black sign was on her breast that bowed,

A broad black band ran down her snow-white shroud;
That lamp she held was her own burning heart,
Whose blood-drops trickled step by step apart;
  The mystery was clear;
  Mad rage had swallowed fear.

As I came through the desert thus it was,
As I came through the desert: By the sea
She knelt and bent above that senseless me;
Those lamp-drops fell upon my white brow there,
She tried to cleanse them with her tears and hair;
She murmured words of pity, love, and woe,
She heeded not the level rushing flow:
  And mad with rage and fear,
  I stood stonebound so near.

As I came through the desert thus it was,
As I came through the desert: When the tide
Swept up to her there kneeling by my side,
She clasped that corpse-like me, and they were borne
Away, and this vile me was left forlorn;
I know the whole sea cannot quench that heart,
Or cleanse that brow, or wash those two apart:
  They love; their doom is drear,
  Yet they nor hope nor fear;
  But I, what do I here?

V

How he arrives there none can clearly know;
  Athwart the mountains and immense wild tracts,
Or flung a waif upon that vast sea-flow,
  Or down the river's boiling cataracts:

To reach it is as dying fever-stricken;
To leave it. slow faint birth intense pangs quicken;
  And memory swoons in both the tragic acts.

But being there one feels a citizen;
  Escape seems hopeless to the heart forlorn:
Can Death-in-Life be brought to life again?
  And yet release does come; there comes a morn
When he awakes from slumbering so sweetly
That all the world is changed for him completely,
  And he is verily as if new-born.

He scarcely can believe the blissful change,
  He weeps perchance who wept not while accurst;
Never again will he approach the range
  Infected by that evil spell now burst:
Poor wretch! who once hath paced that dolent city
Shall pace it often, doomed beyond all pity,
  With horror ever deepening from the first.

Though he possess sweet babes and loving wife,
  A home of peace by loyal friendships cheered,
And love them more than death or happy life,
  They shall avail not; he must dree his weird;
Renounce all blessings for that imprecation,
Steal forth and haunt that builded desolation,
  Of woe and terrors and thick darkness reared.

VI

I sat forlornly by the river-side,
  And watched the bridge-lamps glow like golden stars
Above the blackness of the swelling tide,

Down which they struck rough gold in ruddier bars;
And heard the heave and plashing of the flow
Against the wall a dozen feet below.

Large elm-trees stood along that river-walk;
    And under one, a few steps from my seat,
I heard strange voices join in stranger talk,
    Although I had not heard approaching feet;
These bodiless voices in my waking dream
Flowed dark words blending with the sombre stream: —

And you have after all come back; come back.
I was about to follow on your track.
And you have failed: our spark of hope is black.

That I have failed is proved by my return:
The spark is quenched, nor ever more will burn.
But listen; and the story you shall learn.

I reached the portal common spirits fear,
And read the words above it, dark yet clear,
'Leave hope behind, all ye who enter here:'

And would have passed in, gratified to gain
That positive eternity of pain,
Instead of this insufferable inane.

A demon warder clutched me, Not so fast;
First leave your hopes behind! — But years have passed
Since I left all behind me, to the last:

You cannot count for hope, with all your wit,
This bleak despair that drives me to the Pit:
How could I seek to enter void of it?

He snarled, What thing is this which apes a soul,
And would find entrance to our gulf of dole
Without the payment of the settled toll?

Outside the gate he showed an open chest:
Here pay their entrance fees the souls unblest;
Cast in some hope, you enter with the rest.

This is Pandora's box; whose lid shall shut,
And Hell-gate too, when hopes have filled it; but
They are so thin that it will never glut.

I stood a few steps backwards, desolate;
And watched the spirits pass me to their fate,
And fling off hope, and enter at the gate.

When one casts off a load he springs upright,
Squares back his shoulders, breathes with all his might,
And briskly paces forward strong and light:

But these, as if they took some burden, bowed;
The whole frame sank; however strong and proud
Before, they crept in quite infirm and cowed.

And as they passed me, earnestly from each
A morsel of his hope I did beseech,
To pay my entrance; but all mocked my speech.

Not one would cede a tittle of his store
Though knowing that in instants three or four
He must resign the whole for evermore.

So I returned. Our destiny is fell;
For in this Limbo we must ever dwell,
Shut out alike from Heaven and Earth and Hell.

The other sighed back, Yea; but if we grope
With care through all this Limbo's dreary scope,
We yet may pick up some minute lost hope;

And, sharing it between us, entrance win,
In spite of fiends so jealous for gross sin:
Let us without delay our search begin.

VII

Some say that phantoms haunt those shadowy streets
   And mingle freely there with sparse mankind;
And tell of ancient woes and black defeats,
   And murmur mysteries in the grave enshrined:
But others think them visions of illusion,
Or even men gone far in self-confusion;
   No man there being wholly sane in mind.

And yet a man who raves, however mad,
   Who bares his heart and tells of his own fall,
Reserves some inmost secret good or bad:
   The phantoms have no reticence at all:
The nudity of flesh will blush though tameless,
The extreme nudity of bone grins shameless,
   The unsexed skeleton mocks shroud and pall.

I have seen phantoms there that were as men
   And men that were as phantoms flit and roam;
Marked shapes that were not living to my ken,
   Caught breathings acrid as with Dead Sea foam:
The City rests for man so weird and awful,
That his intrusion there might seem unlawful,
   And phantoms there may have their proper home.

VIII

While I still lingered on that river-walk,
  And watched the tide as black as our black doom,
I heard another couple join in talk,
  And saw them to the left hand in the gloom
Seated against an elm bole on the ground,
Their eyes intent upon the stream profound.

'I never knew another man on earth
  But had some joy or solace in his life,
  Some chance of triumph in the dreadful strife:
My doom has been unmitigated dearth.'

'We gaze upon the river, and we note
The various vessels large and small that float,
Ignoring every wrecked and sunken boat.'

'And yet I asked no splendid dower, no spoil
  Of sway or fame or rank or even wealth;
  But homely love with common food and health,
And nightly sleep to balance daily toil.'

'This all-too humble soul would arrogate
Unto itself some signalising hate
From the supreme indifference of Fate!'
'Who is most wretched in this dolorous place?
  I think myself; yet I would rather be
  My miserable self than He, than He
Who formed such creatures to His own disgrace.

'The vilest thing must be less vile than Thou
  From whom it had its being, God and Lord!
  Creator of all woe and sin! abhorred,

Malignant and implacable! I vow
'That not for all Thy power furled and unfurled,
  For all the temples to Thy glory built,
  Would I assume the ignominious guilt
Of having made such men in such a world.'

'As if a Being, God or Fiend, could reign,
At once so wicked, foolish, and insane,
As to produce men when He might refrain!

'The world rolls round for ever like a mill;
It grinds out death and life and good and ill;
It has no purpose, heart or mind or will.

'While air of Space and Time's full river flow
The mill must blindly whirl unresting so:
It may be wearing out, but who can know?

'Man might know one thing were his sight less dim;
That it whirls not to suit his petty whim,
That it is quite indifferent to him.

'Nay, does it treat him harshly as he saith?
It grinds him some slow years of bitter breath,
Then grinds him back into eternal death.'

IX

It is full strange to him who hears and feels,
  When wandering there in some deserted street,
The booming and the jar of ponderous wheels,
  The trampling clash of heavy ironshod feet:
Who in this Venice of the Black Sea rideth?

Who in this city of the stars abideth
  To buy or sell as those in daylight sweet?
The rolling thunder seems to fill the sky
  As it comes on; the horses snort and strain,
The harness jingles, as it passes by;
  The hugeness of an overburthened wain:
A man sits nodding on the shaft or trudges
Three parts asleep beside his fellow-drudges:
  And so it rolls into the night again.

What merchandise? whence, whither, and for whom?
  Perchance it is a Fate-appointed hearse,
Bearing away to some mysterious tomb
  Or Limbo of the scornful universe
The joy, the peace, the life-hope, the abortions
Of all things good which should have been our portions,
  But have been strangled by that City's curse.

X

The mansion stood apart in its own ground;
  In front thereof a fragrant garden-lawn,
High trees about it, and the whole walled round:
  The massy iron gates were both withdrawn;
And every window of its front shed light,
Portentous in that City of the Night.

But though thus lighted it was deadly still
  As all the countless bulks of solid gloom:
Perchance a congregation to fulfil
  Solemnities of silence in this doom,
Mysterious rites of dolour and despair
Permitting not a breath of chant or prayer?

Broad steps ascended to a terrace broad
  Whereon lay still light from the open door;
The hall was noble, and its aspect awed,
  Hung round with heavy black from dome to floor;
And ample stairways rose to left and right
Whose balustrades were also draped with night.

I paced from room to room, from hall to hall,
  Nor any life throughout the maze discerned;
But each was hung with its funereal pall,
  And held a shrine, around which tapers burned,
With picture or with statue or with bust,
All copied from the same fair form of dust:

A woman very young and very fair;
  Beloved by bounteous life and joy and youth,
And loving these sweet lovers, so that care
  And age and death seemed not for her in sooth:
Alike as stars, all beautiful and bright,
These shapes lit up that mausoléan night.

At length I heard a murmur as of lips,
  And reached an open oratory hung
With heaviest blackness of the whole eclipse;
  Beneath the dome a fuming censer swung;
And one lay there upon a low white bed,
With tapers burning at the foot and head:

The Lady of the images: supine,
  Deathstill, lifesweet, with folded palms she lay:
And kneeling there as at a sacred shrine
  A young man wan and worn who seemed to pray
A crucifix of dim and ghostly white

Surmounted the large altar left in night: —
The chambers of the mansion of my heart,
In every one whereof thine image dwells,
Are black with grief eternal for thy sake.

The inmost oratory of my soul,
Wherein thou ever dwellest quick or dead,
Is black with grief eternal for thy sake.

I kneel beside thee and I clasp the cross,
With eyes for ever fixed upon that face,
So beautiful and dreadful in its calm.

I kneel here patient as thou liest there;
As patient as a statue carved in stone,
Of adoration and eternal grief.

While thou dost not awake I cannot move;
And something tells me thou wilt never wake,
And I alive feel turning into stone.

Most beautiful were Death to end my grief,
Most hateful to destroy the sight of thee,
Dear vision better than all death or life.

But I renounce all choice of life or death,
For either shall be ever at thy side,
And thus in bliss or woe be ever well. —

He murmured thus and thus in monotone,
  Intent upon that uncorrupted face,
Entranced except his moving lips alone:
  I glided with hushed footsteps from the place.
This was the festival that filled with light

That palace in the City of the Night.

XI

What men are they who haunt these fatal glooms,
  And fill their living mouths with dust of death,
And make their habitations in the tombs,
  And breathe eternal sighs with mortal breath,
And pierce life's pleasant veil of various error
To reach that void of darkness and old terror
  Wherein expire the lamps of hope and faith?

They have much wisdom yet they are not wise,
  They have much goodness yet they do not well,
(The fools we know have their own Paradise,
  The wicked also have their proper Hell);
They have much strength but still their doom is stronger,
Much patience but their time endureth longer,
  Much valour but life mocks it with some spell.

They are most rational and yet insane:
  An outward madness not to be controlled;
A perfect reason in the central brain,
  Which has no power, but sitteth wan and cold,
And sees the madness, and foresees as plainly
The ruin in its path, and trieth vainly
  To cheat itself refusing to behold.

And some are great in rank and wealth and power,
  And some renowned for genius and for worth;
And some are poor and mean, who brood and cower
  And shrink from notice, and accept all dearth
Of body, heart and soul, and leave to others
All boons of life: yet these and those are brothers,
  The saddest and the weariest men on earth.

XII

Our isolated units could be brought
  To act together for some common end?
For one by one, each silent with his thought,
  I marked a long loose line approach and wend
Athwart the great cathedral's cloistered square,
And slowly vanish from the moonlit air.

Then I would follow in among the last:
  And in the porch a shrouded figure stood,
Who challenged each one pausing ere he passed,
  With deep eyes burning through a blank white hood:
Whence come you in the world of life and light
To this our City of Tremendous Night? —

From pleading in a senate of rich lords
For some scant justice to our countless hordes
Who toil half-starved with scarce a human right:
I wake from daydreams to his real night.

From wandering through many a solemn scene
Of opium visions, with a heart serene
And intellect miraculously bright:
I wake from daydreams to this real night.

From making hundreds laugh and roar with glee
By my transcendent feats of mimicry,
And humour wanton as an elfish sprite:
I wake from daydreams to this real night.

From prayer and fasting in a lonely cell,
Which brought an ecstasy ineffable

Of love and adoration and delight:
I wake from daydreams to this real night.

From ruling on a splendid kingly throne
A nation which beneath my rule has grown
Year after year in wealth and arts and might:
I wake from daydreams to this real night.

From preaching to an audience fired with faith
The Lamb who died to save our souls from death,
Whose blood hath washed our scarlet sins wool-white:
I wake from daydreams to this real night.

From drinking fiery poison in a den
Crowded with tawdry girls and squalid men,
Who hoarsely laugh and curse and brawl and fight:
I wake from daydreams to this real night.

From picturing with all beauty and all grace
First Eden and the parents of our race,
A luminous rapture unto all men's sight:
I wake from daydreams to this real night.

From writing a great work with patient plan
To justify the ways of God to man,
And show how ill must fade and perish quite:
I wake from daydreams to this real night.

From desperate fighting with a little band
Against the powerful tyrants of our land,
To free our brethren in their own despite:
I wake from daydreams to this real night.

Thus, challenged by that warder sad and stern,

Each one responded with his countersign,
Then entered the cathedral; and in turn
 I entered also, having given mine;
But lingered near until I heard no more,
And marked the closing of the massive door.

XIII

Of all things human which are strange and wild
 This is perchance the wildest and most strange,
And showeth man most utterly beguiled,
 To those who haunt that sunless City's range;
That he bemoans himself for aye, repeating
How time is deadly swift, how life is fleeting,
 How naught is constant on the earth but change.

The hours are heavy on him and the days;
 The burden of the months he scarce can bear;
And often in his secret soul he prays
 To sleep through barren periods unaware,
Arousing at some longed-for date of pleasure;
Which having passed and yielded him small treasure,
 He would outsleep another term of care.

Yet in his marvellous fancy he must make
 Quick wings for Time, and see it fly from us;
This Time which crawleth like a monstrous snake,
 Wounded and slow and very venomous;
Which creeps blindwormlike round the earth and ocean,
Distilling poison at each painful motion,
 And seems condemned to circle ever thus.

And since he cannot spend and use aright

The little time here given him in trust,
But wasteth it in weary undelight
  Of foolish toil and trouble, strife and lust,
He naturally claimeth to inherit
The everlasting Future, that his merit
  May have full scope; as surely is most just.

O length of the intolerable hours,
  O nights that are as aeons of slow pain,
O Time, too ample for our vital powers,
  O Life whose woeful vanities remain
Immutable for all of all our legions
Through all the centuries and in all the regions,
  Not of your speed and variance *we* complain.

We do not ask a longer term of strife,
  Weakness and weariness and nameless woes:
We do not claim renewed and endless life
  When this which is our torment here shall close,
An everlasting conscious inanition!
We yearn for speedy death in full fruition,
  Dateless oblivion and divine repose.

XIV

Large glooms were gathered in the mighty fane,
  With tinted moongleams slanting here and there;
And all was hush: no swelling organ-strain,
  No chant, no voice or murmuring of prayer;
No priests came forth, no tinkling censers fumed,
And the high altar space was unillumed.

Around the pillars and against the walls
  Leaned men and shadows; others seemed to brood

Bent or recumbent in secluded stalls.
  Perchance they were not a great multitude
Save in that city of so lonely streets
Where one may count up every face he meets.
All patiently awaited the event
  Without a stir or sound, as if no less
Self-occupied, doomstricken, while attent.
  And then we heard a voice of solemn stress
From the dark pulpit, and our gaze there met
Two eyes which burned as never eyes burned yet:

Two steadfast and intolerable eyes
  Burning beneath a broad and rugged brow;
The head behind it of enormous size,
  And as black fir-groves in a large wind bow,
Our rooted congregation, gloom-arrayed,
By that great sad voice deep and full were swayed:

O melancholy Brothers, dark, dark, dark!
O battling in black floods without an ark!
  O spectral wanderers of unholy Night!
My soul hath bled for you these sunless years,
With bitter blood-drops running down like tears:
  Oh, dark, dark, dark, withdrawn from joy and light!

My heart is sick with anguish for your bale!
Your woe hath been my anguish; yea, I quail
  And perish in your perishing unblest.
And I have searched the highths and depths, the scope
Of all our universe, with desperate hope
  To find some solace for your wild unrest.

And now at last authentic word I bring,
Witnessed by every dead and living thing;

Good tidings of great joy for you, for all:
There is no God; no Fiend with names divine
Made us and tortures us; if we must pine,
    It is to satiate no Being's gall.
It was the dark delusion of a dream,
That living Person conscious and supreme,
    Whom we must curse for cursing us with life;
Whom we must curse because the life He gave
Could not be buried in the quiet grave,
    Could not be killed by poison or by knife.

This little life is all we must endure,
The grave's most holy peace is ever sure,
    We fall asleep and never wake again;
Nothing is of us but the mouldering flesh,
Whose elements dissolve and merge afresh
    In earth, air, water, plants, and other men.
We finish thus; and all our wretched race
Shall finish with its cycle, and give place
    To other beings, with their own time-doom
Infinite aeons ere our kind began;
Infinite aeons after the last man
    Has joined the mammoth in earth's tomb and womb.

We bow down to the universal laws,
Which never had for man a special clause
    Of cruelty or kindness, love or hate:
If toads and vultures are obscene to sight,
If tigers burn with beauty and with might,
    Is it by favour or by wrath of Fate?

All substance lives and struggles evermore
Through countless shapes continually at war,
    By countless interactions interknit:
If one is born a certain day on earth,

All times and forces tended to that birth,
  Not all the world could change or hinder it.

I find no hint throughout the Universe
Of good or ill, of blessing or of curse;
  I find alone Necessity Supreme;
With infinite Mystery, abysmal, dark,
Unlighted ever by the faintest spark
  For us the flitting shadows of a dream.

O Brothers of sad lives! they are so brief;
A few short years must bring us all relief:
  Can we not bear these years of labouring breath?
But if you would not this poor life fulfil,
Lo, you are free to end it when you will,
  Without the fear of waking after death.—
The organ-like vibrations of his voice
  Thrilled through the vaulted aisles and died away
The yearning of the tones which bade rejoice
  Was sad and tender as a requiem lay:
Our shadowy congregation rested still
As brooding on that 'End it when you will.'

XV

Wherever men are gathered, all the air
  Is charged with human feeling, human thought;
Each shout and cry and laugh, each curse and prayer,
  Are into its vibrations surely wrought;
Unspoken passion, wordless meditation,
Are breathed into it with our respiration;
  It is with our life fraught and overfraught.

So that no man there breathes earth's simple breath,
  As if alone on mountains or wide seas;
But nourishes warm life or hastens death
  With joys and sorrows, health and foul disease,
Wisdom and folly, good and evil labours,
Incessant of his multitudinous neighbours;
  He in his turn affecting all of these.

That City's atmosphere is dark and dense,
  Although not many exiles wander there,
With many a potent evil influence,
  Each adding poison to the poisoned air;
Infections of unutterable sadness,
Infections of incalculable madness,
  Infections of incurable despair.

XVI

Our shadowy congregation rested still,
  As musing on that message we had heard
And brooding on that 'End it when you will;'
  Perchance awaiting yet some other word;
When keen as lightning through a muffled sky
Sprang forth a shrill and lamentable cry: —

The man speaks sooth, alas! the man speaks sooth:
  We have no personal life beyond the grave;
There is no God; Fate knows nor wrath nor ruth:
  Can I find here the comfort which I crave?

In all eternity I had one chance,
  One few years'term of gracious human life:
The splendours of the intellect's advance,

The sweetness of the home with babes and wife;

The social pleasures with their genial wit;
　The fascination of the worlds of art,
The glories of the worlds of nature, lit
　By large imagination's glowing heart;

The rapture of mere being, full of health;
　The careless childhood and the ardent youth,
The strenuous manhood winning various wealth,
　The reverend age serene with life's long truth:

All the sublime prerogatives of Man;
　The storied memories of the times of old,
The patient tracking of the world's great plan
　Through sequences and changes myriadfold.

This chance was never offered me before;
　For me the infinite Past is blank and dumb:
This chance recurreth never, nevermore;
　Blank, blank for me the infinite To-come.

And this sole chance was frustrate from my birth,
　A mockery, a delusion; and my breath
Of noble human life upon this earth
　So racks me that I sigh for senseless death.

My wine of life is poison mixed with gall,
　My noonday passes in a nightmare dream,
I worse than lose the years which are my all:
　What can console me for the loss supreme?

Speak not of comfort where no comfort is,
　Speak not at all: can words make foul things fair?

Our life's a cheat, our death a black abyss:
  Hush and be mute envisaging despair. —

This vehement voice came from the northern aisle
  Rapid and shrill to its abrupt harsh close;
And none gave answer for a certain while,
  For words must shrink from these most wordless woes;
At last the pulpit speaker simply said,
With humid eyes and thoughtful drooping head: —

My Brother, my poor Brothers, it is thus;
This life itself holds nothing good for us,
  But it ends soon and nevermore can be;
And we knew nothing of it ere our birth,
And shall know nothing when consigned to earth:
  I ponder these thoughts and they comfort me.

XVII

How the moon triumphs through the endless nights!
  How the stars throb and glitter as they wheel
Their thick processions of supernal lights
  Around the blue vault obdurate as steel!
And men regard with passionate awe and yearning
The mighty marching and the golden burning,
  And think the heavens respond to what they feel.

Boats gliding like dark shadows of a dream,
  Are glorified from vision as they pass
The quivering moonbridge on the deep black stream;
  Cold windows kindle their dead glooms of glass
To restless crystals; cornice, dome, and column
Emerge from chaos in the splendour solemn;

Like faëry lakes gleam lawns of dewy grass.

With such a living light these dead eyes shine,
  These eyes of sightless heaven, that as we gaze
We read a pity, tremulous, divine,
  Or cold majestic scorn in their pure rays:
Fond man! they are not haughty, are not tender;
There is no heart or mind in all their splendour,
  They thread mere puppets all their marvellous maze.

If we could near them with the flight unflown,
  We should but find them worlds as sad as this,
Or suns all self-consuming like our own
  Enringed by planet worlds as much amiss:
They wax and wane through fusion and confusion;
The spheres eternal are a grand illusion,
  The empyréan is a void abyss.

XVIII

I wandered in a suburb of the north,
  And reached a spot whence three close lanes led down,
Beneath thick trees and hedgerows winding forth
  Like deep brook channels, deep and dark and lown:
The air above was wan with misty light,
The dull grey south showed one vague blur of white.

I took the left-hand lane and slowly trod
  Its earthen footpath, brushing as I went
The humid leafage; and my feet were shod
  With heavy languor, and my frame downbent,
With infinite sleepless weariness outworn,

So many nights I thus had paced forlorn.

After a hundred steps I grew aware
  Of something crawling in the lane below;
It seemed a wounded creature prostrate there
  That sobbed with pangs in making progress slow,
The hind limbs stretched to push, the fore limbs then
To drag; for it would die in its own den.

But coming level with it I discerned
  That it had been a man; for at my tread
It stopped in its sore travail and half-turned,
  Leaning upon its right, and raised its head,
And with the left hand twitched back as in ire
Long grey unreverend locks befouled with mire.

A haggard filthy face with bloodshot eyes,
  An infamy for manhood to behold.
He gasped all trembling, What, you want my prize?
  You leave, to rob me, wine and lust and gold
And all that men go mad upon, since you
Have traced my sacred secret of the clue?

You think that I am weak and must submit;
  Yet I but scratch you with this poisoned blade,
And you are dead as if I clove with it
  That false fierce greedy heart. Betrayed! Betrayed!
I fling this phial if you seek to pass,
And you are forthwith shrivelled up like grass.

And then with sudden change, Take thought! take thought!
  Have pity on me! it is mine alone.
If you could find, it would avail you naught;
  Seek elsewhere on the pathway of your own:

For who of mortal or immortal race
The lifetrack of another can retrace?

Did you but know my agony and toil!
  Two lanes diverge up yonder from this lane;
My thin blood marks the long length of their soil;
  Such clue I left, who sought my clue in vain:
My hands and knees are worn both flesh and bone;
I cannot move but with continual moan.
But I am in the very way at last
  To find the long-lost broken golden thread
Which reunites my present with my past,
  If you but go your own way. And I said,
I will retire as soon as you have told
Whereunto leadeth this lost thread of gold.

And so you know it not! he hissed with scorn;
  I feared you, imbecile! It leads me back
From this accursed night without a morn,
  And through the deserts which have else no track,
And through vast wastes of horror-haunted time,
To Eden innocence in Eden's clime:

And I become a nursling soft and pure,
  An infant cradled on its mother's knee,
Without a past, love-cherished and secure;
  Which if it saw this loathsome present Me,
Would plunge its face into the pillowing breast,
And scream abhorrence hard to lull to rest.

He turned to grope; and I retiring brushed
  Thin shreds of gossamer from off my face,
And mused, His life would grow, the germ uncrushed;
  He should to antenatal night retrace,

And hide his elements in that large womb
Beyond the reach of man-evolving Doom.

And even thus, what weary way were planned,
  To seek oblivion through the far-off gate
Of birth, when that of death is close at hand!
  For this is law, if law there be in Fate:
What never has been, yet may have its when;
The thing which has been, never is again.

XIX

The mighty river flowing dark and deep,
  With ebb and flood from the remote sea-tides
Vague-sounding through the City's sleepless sleep,
  Is named the River of the Suicides;
For night by night some lorn wretch overweary,
And shuddering from the future yet more dreary,
  Within its cold secure oblivion hides.

One plunges from a bridge's parapet,
  As by some blind and sudden frenzy hurled;
Another wades in slow with purpose set
  Until the waters are above him furled;
Another in a boat with dreamlike motion
Glides drifting down into the desert ocean,
  To starve or sink from out the desert world.

They perish from their suffering surely thus,
  For none beholding them attempts to save,
The while each thinks how soon, solicitous,
  He may seek refuge in the self-same wave;
Some hour when tired of ever-vain endurance

Impatience will forerun the sweet assurance
   Of perfect peace eventual in the grave.

When this poor tragic-farce has palled us long,
   Why actors and spectators do we stay? —
To fill our so-short *rôles* out right or wrong;
   To see what shifts are yet in the dull play
For our illusion; to refrain from grieving
Dear foolish friends by our untimely leaving:
   But those asleep at home, how blest are they!

Yet it is but for one night after all:
   What matters one brief night of dreary pain?
When after it the weary eyelids fall
   Upon the weary eyes and wasted brain;
And all sad scenes and thoughts and feelings vanish.
In that sweet sleep no power can ever banish,
   That one best sleep which never wakes again.

XX

I sat me weary on a pillar's base,
   And leaned against the shaft; for broad moonlight
O'erflowed the peacefulness of cloistered space,
   A shore of shadow slanting from the right:
The great cathedral's western front stood there,
A wave-worn rock in that calm sea of air.

Before it, opposite my place of rest,
   Two figures faced each other, large, austere;
A couchant sphinx in shadow to the breast,
   An angel standing in the moonlight clear;
So mighty by magnificence of form,

They were not dwarfed beneath that mass enorm.

Upon the cross-hilt of a naked sword
   The angel's hands, as prompt to smite, were held;
His vigilant intense regard was poured
   Upon the creature placidly unquelled,
Whose front was set at level gaze which took
No heed of aught, a solemn trance-like look.

And as I pondered these opposèd shapes
   My eyelids sank in stupor, that dull swoon
Which drugs and with a leaden mantle drapes
   The outworn to worse weariness. But soon
A sharp and clashing noise the stillness broke,
And from the evil lethargy I woke.

The angel's wings had fallen, stone on stone,
   And lay there shattered; hence the sudden sound:
A warrior leaning on his sword alone
   Now watched the sphinx with that regard profound;
The sphinx unchanged looked forthright, as aware
Of nothing in the vast abyss of air.

Again I sank in that repose unsweet,
   Again a clashing noise my slumber rent;
The warrior's sword lay broken at his feet:
   An unarmed man with raised hands impotent
Now stood before the sphinx, which ever kept
Such mien as if with open eyes it slept.

My eyelids sank in spite of wonder grown;
   A louder crash upstartled me in dread:
The man had fallen forward, stone on stone,
   And lay there shattered, with his trunkless head

Between the monster's large quiescent paws,
Beneath its grand front changeless as life's laws.
The moon had circled westward full and bright,
    And made the temple-front a mystic dream.
And bathed the whole enclosure with its light,
    The sworded angel's wrecks, the sphinx supreme
I pondered long that cold majestic face
Whose vision seemed of infinite void space.

XXI

Anear the centre of that northern crest
    Stands out a level upland bleak and bare,
From which the city east and south and west
    Sinks gently in long waves; and thronèd there
An Image sits, stupendous, superhuman,
The bronze colossus of a wingèd Woman,
    Upon a graded granite base foursquare.

Low-seated she leans forward massively,
    With cheek on clenched left hand, the forearm's might
Erect, its elbow on her rounded knee;
    Across a clasped book in her lap the right
Upholds a pair of compasses; she gazes
With full set eyes, but wandering in thick mazes
    Of sombre thought beholds no outward sight.

Words cannot picture her; but all men know
    That solemn sketch the pure sad artist wrought
Three centuries and threescore years ago,
    With phantasies of his peculiar thought:
The instruments of carpentry and science
Scattered about her feet, in strange alliance

With the keen wolf-hound sleeping undistraught;

Scales, hour-glass, bell, and magic-square above;
    The grave and solid infant perched beside,
With open winglets that might bear a dove,
    Intent upon its tablets, heavy-eyed;
Her folded wings as of a mighty eagle,
But all too impotent to lift the regal
    Robustness of her earth-born strength and pride;

And with those wings, and that light wreath which seems
    To mock her grand head and the knotted frown
Of forehead charged with baleful thoughts and dreams,
    The household bunch of keys, the housewife's gown
Voluminous, indented, and yet rigid
As if a shell of burnished metal frigid;
    The feet thick shod to tread all weakness down;

The comet hanging o'er the waste dark seas,
    The massy rainbow curved in front of it,
Beyond the village with the masts and trees;
    The snaky imp, dog-headed, from the Pit,
Bearing upon its batlike leathern pinions
Her name unfolded in the sun's dominions,
    The 'MELENCOLIA' that transcends all wit.

Thus has the artist copied her, and thus
    Surrounded to expound her form sublime,
Her fate heroic and calamitous;
    Fronting the dreadful mysteries of Time,
Unvanquished in defeat and desolation,
Undaunted in the hopeless conflagration
    Of the day setting on her baffled prime.

Baffled and beaten back she works on still,
   Weary and sick of soul she works the more,
Sustained by her indomitable will:
   The hands shall fashion and the brain shall pore
And all her sorrow shall be turned to labour,
Till death the friend-foe piercing with his sabre
   That mighty heart of hearts ends bitter war.

But as if blacker night could dawn on night,
   With tenfold gloom on moonless night unstarred,
A sense more tragic than defeat and blight,
   More desperate than strife with hope debarred,
More fatal than the adamantine Never
Encompassing her passionate endeavour,
   Dawns glooming in her tenebrous regard:

The sense that every struggle brings defeat
   Because Fate holds no prize to crown success;
That all the oracles are dumb or cheat
   Because they have no secret to express;
That none can pierce the vast black veil uncertain
Because there is no light beyond the curtain;
   That all is vanity and nothingness.

Titanic from her high throne in the north,
   That City's sombre Patroness and Queen,
In bronze sublimity she gazes forth
   Over her Capital of teen and threne,
Over the river with its isles and bridges,
The marsh and moorland, to the stern rock-ridges,
   Confronting them with a coëval mien.

The moving moon and stars from east to west
   Circle before her in the sea of air;

Shadows and gleams glide round her solemn rest.
   Her subjects often gaze up to her there:
The strong to drink new strength of iron endurance,
The weak new terrors; all, renewed assurance
   And confirmation of the old despair.

Other poems

Weddah and Om-El-Bonain

NOTE.—I found this story, which merits a far better English version than I have been able to accomplish, in the *De L' Amour* of De Stendhal (Henri Beyle, chap. 53), where they are given among 'Fragments Extracted and Translated from an Arabic Collection, entitled *The Divan of Love*, compiled by Ebn-Abi-Hadglat.' From another of these fragments I quote a few lines by way of introduction:
'The Benou-Azra are a tribe famous for love among all the tribes of Arabia. So that the manner in which they love has passed into a proverb, and God has not made any other creatures so tender in loving as are they. Sahid, son of Agba, one day asked an Arab, Of what people art thou? I am of the people who die when they love, answered the Arab. Thou art then of the tribe of Azra? said Sahid. Yes, by the master of the Caaba! replied the Arab. Whence comes it, then, that you thus love? asked Sahid. Our women are beautiful and our young men are chaste, answered the Arab.'

On this theme Heine has a poem of four unrhymed quatrains, *Der Azra*, of which the sense without the melody may be given in English:

Daily went the wondrous-lovely
Sultan's daughter to and fro there
In the evening by the fountain,
Where the waters white were plashing.

Daily stood the youthful captive
In the evening by the fountain,
Where the waters white were plashing;
Daily grew he pale and paler.

And one evening the princess
Stepped to him with sudden question:
'I would know your name, young captive,
And your country and your kindred.'

Then the slave replied: 'My name is
Mohammed, I come from Yemen,
And my kindred are the Azra,
They who perish when they love.'

PART I.

I

WEDDAH and Om-el-Bonain, scarcely grown
To boy and girlhood from their swaddling bands,
Were known where'er the Azra tribe was known,
Through Araby and all the neighbouring lands;
Were chanted in the songs of sweetest tone
Which sprang like fountains 'mid the desert sands:
  They were so beautiful that none who saw
  But felt a rapture trembling into awe.

II

Once on a dewy evetide when the balm
Of herb and flower made all the air rich wine,
And still the sunless shadow of the palm
Sought out the birthplace of the day divine,
These two were playing in the happy calm.
A young chief said: In these be sure a sign
  Great God vouchsafes; a living talisman
  Of glory and rich weal to bless our clan.

III

Proud hearts applauded; but a senior chief
Said: Perfect beauty is its own sole end;
It is ripe flower and fruit, not bud and leaf;
The promise and the blessing meet and blend,
Fulfilled at once: then malice, wrath, and grief,
Lust of the foe and passion of the friend,
  Assail the marvel; for all Hell is moved
  Against the work of Allah most approved.

IV

Thus beauty is that pearl a poor man found;
Which could not be surrendered, changed, or sold,
Which he might never bury in the ground,
Or hide away within his girdle-fold;
But had to wear upon his brow uncrowned,
A star of storm and terrors; for, behold,
  The richest kings raged jealous for its light,
  And just men's hearts turned robbers at the sight.

V

But if the soul be royal as the gem,
That star of danger may flash victory too,
The younger urged, and bring the diadern
To set itself in. And the other: True;
If all Life's golden apples crown one stem,
Fate touches none; but single they are few:
  And whether to defeat or triumph, this
  One star lights war and woe, not peaceful bliss.

VI

But nothing recked the children in that hour,
And little recked through fifteen happy years,
Of any doom in their surpassing dower:
Rich with the present, free from hopes and fears,
They dwelt in time as in a heavenly bower:
Their life was strange to laughter as to tears,
  Serenely glad; their partings were too brief
  For pain; and side by side, what thing was grief?

VII

Amidst their clan they dwelt in solitude,
Not haughtily but by instinctive love;
As lion mates with lion in the wood,
And eagle pairs with eagle not with dove;
The lowlier creatures finding their own good
In their own race, nor seeking it above:
  These dreamt as little of divided life
  As that first pair created man and wife.

VIII

The calm years flowed thus till the youth and maid
Were almost man and woman, and the spell
Of passion wrought, and each was self-dismayed;
The hearts their simple childhood knew so well
Were now such riddles to them, in the shade
And trouble of the mists that seethe and swell
  When the large dawn is kindling, which shall grow
  Through crimson fires to steadfast azure glow.

IX

That year a tribe-feud, which some years had slept
Through faintness, woke up stronger than before;
And with its stir young hearts on all sides leapt
For battle, swoln with peace and plenteous store;
Swift couriers to and fro the loud land swept
Weaving thin spites to one vast woof of war:
  And Weddah sallied forth elate, ranked man,
  A warrior of the warriors of his clan.

X

Ere long flushed foes turned haggard at his name;
The beautiful, the terrible: for fire
Burns most intensely in the clearest flame;
The comeliest steed is ever last to tire
And swiftest footed; and in war's fierce game
The noblest sword is deadliest in its gyre:
  His gentle gravity grew keen and gay
  In hottest fight as for a festal day.

XI

And while he fought far distant with his band,
Walid the Syrian, Abd-el-Malek's son;
Renowned already for a scheme long planned
With silent patience, and a sharp deed done
When its ripe fruit leaned ready for his hand,
And liberal sharing of the fruit well won;
  Came south to greet the tribe, and knit anew
  Old bonds of friendship and alliance true.

XII

He had full often from the poets heard
Of these two children the divinely fair;
But was not one to kindle at a word,
And languish on faint echoes of an air;
By what he saw and touched his heart was stirred
Nor knew sick longings and the vague despair
  Of those who turn from every nearest boon
  To catch like infants at the reachless moon.

XIII

But when one sunset flaming crimson-barred
He saw a damsel like a shape of sleep,
Who moved as moves in indolence the pard;
Above whose veil burned large eyes black and deep,
The lairs of an intense and slow regard
Which made all splendours of the broad world cheap,
  And death and life thin dreams; fate-smitten there
  He rested shuddering past the hour of prayer.

XIV

Be heaven all stars, we feel the one moon's rise:
Who else could move with that imperial grace?
Who else could bear about those fateful eyes,
Too overwhelming for a mortal face?
Beyond all heed of questions and surprise
He stood a termless hour in that same place,
  Convulsed in silent wrestling with his doom;
  Haggard as one brought living from the tomb.

XV

And she had shuddered also passing by,
A moment; for her spirit though intent
Was chilled as conscious of an evil eye;
But forthwith turned and o'er its one dream bent;
A woman lilting as she came anigh:
But to destroy on earth was Weddah sent;
  There where he is brave warriors fall before him.
  Where he is not pine damsels who adore him.

XVI

And thus with purpose like a trenchant blade
Forged in that fierce hour's fire, the Syrian chief
Began new life. When next the Council weighed
The heavy future charged with wrath and grief,
He spoke his will: I ask to wed the maid,
The child of Abd-el-Aziz: and, in brief,
  I bring for dowry all our wealth and might,
  Unto our last heart's blood, to fight your fight.

XVII

All mute with marvelling sat. Her sire then said:
From infancy unto my brother's son
She has been held betrothed: our lord can wed
Full many a lovelier, many a richer one.
But quite in vain they reasoned, flattered, pled;
This was his proffer, other he had none:
  A boy and girl outweighed the Azra tribe?
  'Twas strange! His vow was fixed to that sole bribe.

XVIII

And as their couriers came in day by day
Pregnant with portents of yet blacker ill;
And all their urgence broke in fuming spray
Against the rock of his firm-planted will;
The baffled current took a tortuous way,
And drowned a happy garden green and still,
  O'erwhelming Abd-el-Aziz with that gibe,
  A boy and girl outvalue all our tribe?

XIX

He loved his daughter, and he loved yet more
His brothers son; and now the whole tribe prest
The scale against them: there was raging war,
Too sure of hapless issue in his breast;
Sea-tossed where rocks on all sides fanged the shore.
She heard him moaning: Would I were at rest,
  Ere this should come upon me, in the grave!
  Her poor heart bled to hear him weep and rave.

XX

She flung herself all yearning at his feet;
The long white malehair dashed her brow with tears;
But her tears scalded him; her kisses sweet
Were crueller than iron barbs of spears:
He had no eyes her tender eyes to meet;
Her soft caressing words scarce touched his ears
  But they were fire and madness in his brain:
  Yet while she clasped he mutely clasped again.

XXI

At length he answered her: A heavy doom
Is laid upon me; now, when I am old,
And weak, and bending toward the quiet tomb …
Can it then be, as we are sometimes told,
That women, nay, that young girls in their bloom,
Lovely, beloved, and loving, have been bold
  To give their lives, when blenched the bravest man,
  For safety of their city or their clan?

XXII

She trembled in cold shadow of a rock
Leaning to crush her where she knelt fast bound;
She grew all ear to catch the coming shock,
And felt already quakings of the ground;
Yet firmly said: Your anguish would not mock
Your daughter, O my Father: pray expound
  The woeful riddle; and whate'er my part,
  It is your very blood which feeds this heart.

XXIII

He told her all: the perils great and near;
The might of Walid; and the friendship long
Which bound them to his house, and year by year
With mutual kindnesses had grown more strong
His offer, his demand, which would nor hear
A word in mitigation right or wrong.
  Her young blood curdled: Bring him to our tent,
  That I may plead; perchance he will relent.

XXIV

He came; and found her sitting double-veiled,
For grief was round her like a funeral stole.
She pleaded, she o'erwhelmed him, and she failed;
For still the more her passion moved his soul,
The more he loved her; when his heart most quailed,
His purpose stretched most eager for the goal:
  I stake myself, house, friends, all, for the tribe
  Which gives me you; but for no meaner bribe.

XXV

So her face set into a stony mask,
And heavy silence crushed them for an hour
Ere she could learn the words to say her task:
Let only mutes appeal to Fate's deaf power!
Behold I pledge myself to what you ask,
My sire here sells me for the settled dower:
  The sheikhs can know we are at one; I pray
  That none else know it ere the wedding-day.

XXVI

Which shall be when next moon is on the wane
As this to-night: my heart is now the bier
Of that which we have sacrificed and slain;
My own poor Past, still beautiful and dear,
Cut off from life, wants burial; and though vain
Is woman's weeping, I must weep I fear
  A little on the well-beloved's tomb
  Ere marriage smiles and blushes can outbloom.

XXVII

He left them, sire and daughter, to their woe;
Himself then sick at heart as they could be:
But set to work at once, and spurred the slow
Sad hours till they were fiery-swift as he:
With messengers on all sides to and fro,
With ravelled webs of subtle policy,
  He gave the sheikhs good earnest of what aid
  They had so cheaply bought with one fair maid.

XXVIII

Thus he took Araby's one peerless prize,
And homeward went ungrudging all the cost;
Though she was marble; with blank arid eyes,
Weary and hopeless as the waste they crossed
When neither moon nor star is in the skies,
And water faileth, and the track is lost.
  He took such statue triumphing for wife,
  Assured his love would kindle it to life.

XXIX

She had indeed wept, wept and wailed that moon,
But had not buried yet her shrouded Past;
Which ever lay in a most deathlike swoon,
Pallid and pulseless, motionless and ghast,
While Fate withheld from it death's perfect boon:
She kept this doleful mystery locked up fast;
  Her form was as its sepulchre of stone,
  Her heart its purple couch and hidden throne.

XXX

She went; and sweeter voiced than cooing dove
Hassan the bard his farewell ode must render:
We had a Night, the dream of heaven above,
Wherein one moon and countless stars of splendour;
We had a Moon, the face of perfect love,
Wherein two nights with stars more pure and tender:
  Our Night with its one moon we still have here;
  Where is our Moon with its twin nights more dear?

PART II.

I

As Weddah and his troop were coming back
From their first foray, which success made brief,
Scouts met him and in sharp haste turned his track
On special mission to a powerful chief,
Who wavered still between the white and black,
And lurked for mere self-profit like a thief.
  This errand well fulfilled, at last he came
  To flush her tear-pearls with the ruby fame.

II

Into the camp full joyously he rode,
Leading his weary escort; as for him,
The love and trust that in his bosom glowed
Had laughed away all weariness of limb.
The sheikhs, his full report heard, all bestowed
Well-measured praises, brief and somewhat grim;
  As veterans scanning the enormous night
  In which this one star shone so bravely bright.

III

Then Abd-el-Aziz rose and left the tent,
And he accompanied with eager pace;
And marked not how his frank smiles as he went
Were unreflected in each well-known face;
How joyous greetings he on all sides sent
Brought hollow echoes as from caverned space:
  His heart drank sweet wine 'mid the roses singing,
  And thought the whole world with like revels ringing.

IV

He entered with his uncle, and his glance
Sank disappointed. But the old man wept
With passion o'er him, eyeing him askance;
And made him eat and drink; and ever kept
Questioning, questioning, as to every chance
Throughout his absence; keen to intercept
  The fatal, But my cousin? ready strung
  Upon the tense lips by the eager tongue.

V

At length it flew, the lover's wingèd dart;
He sped it wreathed with flowers of hope and joy,
It pierced with iron point the old man's heart,
Who quivering cried: You are, then, still a boy!
Love, love, the sweet to meet, the smart to part,
Make all your world of pleasure and annoy!
  Is this a time for dalliance in rose bowers?
  The vultures gather; do they scent sweet flowers?

VI

It is a time of woe and shame, of strife
Whose victory must be dolorous as defeat:
The sons of Ishmael clutch the stranger's knife
To stab each other; every corpse you meet
Has held a Moslem soul, an Arab life:
The town-serfs prisoned in stark fort and street
  Exult while countless tents that freely roam
  Perish like proud ships clashing in the foam.

VII

We might learn wisdom from our foes and thralls!
The mongrels of a hundred barbarous races,
Who know not their own sires, appease their brawls,
Leave night and sunward set their impure faces,
To bay in concert round old Syrian walls,
And thrust their three gods on our holy places:
  We have one Sire, one Prophet, and one Lord,
  And yet against each other turn the sword.

VIII

Thus long he groaned with fevered bitterness,
Till, Say at least, my Father, she is well!
Stung prudence out of patience: Surely yes!
The children of the faith whom Azrael
Hath gathered, do they suffer our distress?
But smitten by that word the lover fell,
  As if at such rash mention of his name
  That bird of God with wings of midnight came.

IX

Deep in the shadow of those awful plumes
A night and day and night he senseless lay;
And Abd-el-Aziz cowered 'mid deeper glooms,
Silent in vast despair, both night and day:
It seemed two forms belonging to the tombs
Had been abandoned in that tent; for they
  Were stark and still and mute alike, although
  The one was conscious of their double woe.

X

At last death left the balance, and the scale
Of wretched life jarred earth: and in the morn
The lover woke, confused as if a veil
Of heavy dreams involved him; weak and worn
And cold at heart, and wondering what bale
Had wounded him and left him thus forlorn:
  So still half-stunned with anguish he lay long,
  Fretful to rend the shroud that wrapt his wrong.

XI

He turned; and on the pillow, near his head,
He saw a toy, a trifle, that gave tongue
To mute disaster: forthwith on his bed
The coiled-snake Memory hissed and sprang and stung:
Then all the fury of the storm was shed
From the black swollen clouds that overhung;
  The hot rain poured, the fierce gusts shook his soul
  Wild flashes lit waste gloom from pole to pole.

XII

He hardly dared to touch the petty thing,
The talisman of this tremendous spell:
A purse of dark blue silk; a golden ring,
A letter in the hand he knew so well.
Still as he sought to read new gusts would fling
Wet blindness in his vision, and a knell
  Of rushing thunder trample through his brain
  And tread him down into the swoon again.

XIII

He read: Farewell! In one sad word I weave
More thoughts than pen could write or tongue declare.
No other word can Om-el-Bonain leave
To Weddah, save her blessing; and her prayer,
That he will quail not, though his heart must grieve,
That all his strength and valour, skill and care,
  Shall be devoted loyally to serve
  The sacred Tribe, and never self-ward swerve.

XIV

For verily the Tribe is all, and we
Are nothing singly save as parts of it:
The one great Nile flows ever to the sea,
The waterdrops for ever change and flit;
And some the first ooze snares, and some may be
The King's sweet draught, proud Cairo's mirror; fit
  For all each service of the stream whose fame
  They share, by which alone they have a name.

XV

And since I know that you cannot forget,
And am too sure your love will never change,
I leave my image to your soul: but yet
Keep it as shrined and shrouded till the strange
Sad dream of life, illusion and regret,
Is ended; short must be its longest range.
  Farewell! Hope gleams the wan lamp in a tomb
  Above a corpse that waits the final doom.

XVI

This writing was a dear but cruel friend
That dragged him from the deep, and held him fast
Upon life's shore, who would have found an end,
Peace and oblivion. Turn from such a past
To such a future, and unquailing wend
Its infinite hopeless hours! he shrank aghast:
  Yet in this utmost weakness swore to make
  The dreadful sacrifice for her dear sake.

XVII

But when he stood as one about to fall,
And would go weep upon her tomb alone,
And Abd-el-Aziz had to tell him all,
The cry of anguish took a harsher tone;
Rich harem coverlets for funeral pall,
For grave a Syrian marriage couch and throne!
  A human rival, breathing mortal breath,
  And not the star-cold sanctity of Death!

XVIII

This truth was as a potent poison-draught,
Fire in the entrails, wild fire in the brain,
Which kindled savage strength in him who quaffed
And did not die of its first maddening pain.
It struck him like the mere malignant shaft
Which stings a warrior into sense again,
  Who lay benumbed with wounds, and would have died
  Unroused: the fresh wound makes him crawl and hide.

XIX

A month he wandered in wild solitude;
And in that month grew old, and yet grew strong:
Now lying prone and still as death would brood
The whole long day through and the whole night long;
Now demon-driven day and night pursued
Stark weariness amidst the clamorous throng
  Of thoughts that raged with memory and desire,
  And parched, his bruised feet burning, could not tire.

XX

When he came back, o'ermastered by his vow
To serve the Tribe through which he was unblest,
None gazed without remorse upon his brow,
None felt his glance without an aching breast:
Magnificent in beauty even now,
Ravaged by grief and fury and unrest,
  He moved among them swift and stern of deed,
  And always silent save in action's need.

XXI

And thus went forth, and unrejoicingly
Drank deep of war's hot wine: as one who drinks
And only grows more sullen, while yet he
Never the challenge of the full cup shrinks;
And rises pale with horror when the glee
Of careless revellers into slumber sinks,
  Because the feast which could not give him joy
  At least kept phantoms from their worst annoy.

XXII

The lion of the Azra is come back
A meagre wolf! foes mocked, who mocked no more
When midnight scared them with his fresh attack
After the long day's fighting, and the war
Found him for ever wolf-like on their track,
As if consumed with slakeless thirst of gore:
  Since he was cursed from slumber and repose,
  He wreaked his restlessness on friends and foes.

XXIII

The lightnings of his keen sword ever flashed
Without a ray of lightning in his glance;
His blade where blades were thickest clove or clashed
Without a war-cry: ever in advance
He sought out death; but death as if abashed
Adopted for its own his sword and lance,
  And rode his steed, and swayed aside or blunted
  The eager hostile weapons he affronted.

XXIV

Once in the thick of battle as he raged
Thus cold and dumb amidst the furious cries,
Hassan the bard was near to him engaged,
And read a weird in those forlorn fixed eyes;
And singing of that combat they had waged
Gave voice to what surpassed his own surmise:
 For our young Lion of the mateless doom
 Shall never go a cold corpse to the tomb!

XXX

Awe silenced him who sang, and deep awe fell
On those who heard it round the campfire's blaze:
But when they questioned he had nought to tell;
The vision had departed from his gaze.
The verse took wing and was a mighty spell;
Upon the foe new terror and amaze,
  To friends redoubled force; to one alone,
  The hero's self, it long remained unknown.

XXVI

While Weddah in the South with fiery will
Bore conquest wheresoe'er his banner flew,
Walid with royal heart and patient skill
Upon the Syrian confines triumphed too.
They never met: each felt a savage thrill
Which jarred his inmost being through and through
  As still fresh fame the other's fame enlarged:
  Each wished his rival in the ranks he charged.

XXVII

And when the foemen sued at length for peace
To victors surfeited with war's alarms,
Save him who knew all rest in rest must cease,
They said: O warriors, not by your own arms,
Though they are mighty! may their might increase!
But more by Om-el-Bonain's fatal charms,
  Possessing both who lost her and who won,
   Have we been baffled, vanquished, and undone.

XXVIII

Whence Hassan sang his sudden daring ode
Of Beauty revelling in the storm of fight:
For if the warriors into battle rode,
Their hearts were kindled by her living light;
Either as sun that in pure azure glowed,
Or baleful star in deep despair's black night:
  And whether by despair or joy she lit
   Intenser fires perplexed the poet's wit.

XXIX

And would you know why empires break asunder,
Why peoples perish and proud cities fall;
Seek not the captains where the steel clouds thunder,
Seek not the elders in the council hall;
But seek the chamber where some shining wonder
Of delicate beauty nestles, far from all
  The turmoil, toying with adornments queenly,
   And murmuring songs of tender love serenely.

XXX

The clashing cymbals and the trumpet's clangour
Are peacefuller than her soft trembling lute;
The armies raging with hot fire of anger
Are gentler than her gentle glances mute;
The restless rushings of her dainty languor
Outveer the wind, outspeed the barb's pursuit:
  Well Hassan knows; who sings high laud and blessing
  To this dear fatal riddle past all guessing.

PART III.

I

The war was over for the time: and men
Returned to heal its wounds, repair its waste,
And thus grow strong and rich to fight again.
And Weddah, cold in victory's sun, embraced
The uncle whom his glory warmed; and then
Gathering his spoil of gems and gold in haste,
  Rode forth: the clansmen wondered much to find
  His famous favourite steed was left behind.

II

He set out in the night: none knew his goal,
Though some might fix it in their secret thought.
He could no longer stifle or control,
In calm by battle's fever undistraught,
The piteous yearning of his famished soul
Which unappeasably its food besought;
  Fretting his life out like an infant's cry,
  Let us but see her once before we die!

III

When he returned not, soon the rumour spread;
That he had vanished now his work was done:
The prophecy had been fulfilled; not dead
But in the body borne beyond the sun,
He lived eternal life. He heard this said
Himself in Walid's city, where as one
  Who sojourns but for traffic's sake he dwelt;
  And hearing it, more surely shrouded felt.

IV

Courteous and humble as beseemeth trade,
While ever on the watch, some gems he sold:
Men said, this young man is discreet and staid
Yet fair in dealing, nor too fond of gold.
He smiled to hear his virtues thus arrayed,
A smile that gloomed to frowning; but controlled
  The haughty spirit surging in his breast;
  The end in view, what mattered all the rest?

V

The end in reach: for now the favourite slave
Of Om-el-Bonain, as he knew full well;
A frank-eyed girl, whose bosom was a wave
Whereon love's lotus lightly rose and fell;
Drew near to him, attracted by his grave
Unsceptred majesty, and by the spell
  Of his intense and fathomless regard,
  Splendid in gloom as midnight myriad-starred.

VI

She haggled for a trinket with her tongue
To veil the eager commerce of her eyes;
Those daring smugglers when the heart is young,
For contraband of passion. His disguise
In talk with her but loosely round him hung;
She glimpsed a secret and an enterprise;
  Love's flower, unsunned by hope, soon fades; she grieves,
  Yet still returns to scent the rich dead leaves.

VII

Till sick at heart and desperate with delay
He ventured all, abruptly flinging down
The weary mask: if death must end the play
Better at once: I learn that in your town
Dwells Om-el-Bonain, whom you know men say.
Upon her eye-flash dropped a decent frown:
  She is my mistress, and great Walid's wife —
  The word his heart sought, stabbed in with a knife.

VIII

Your mistress is my cousin; and will be
The friend of who shall tell her I am here.
But if I may not trust your secrecy,
Tell Walid, tell not her: and have no fear
That I will harm you for harm done to me,
Unaimed at her. The life I hold not dear
  Might dower you well. But with a passionate oath
  The eager girl swore loyalty to both.

IX

Then hurried from him to her lady sweet,
And thrilled her frozen heart with burning pang:
For life resigned and torpid in defeat
To new contention with its fate upsprang,
This sword of hope found lying at her feet
While love's impetuous clarion summons rang:
  Weddah alive: alive and here! Beware!
  If you now mock, Hell mock your dying prayer!

X

I saw a merchant: never chief or king
Of form so noble visited our land;
He wore a little ring, a lady's ring,
On the last finger of a feared right hand;
Some woe enormous overshadowing
Made beauty terrible that had been bland;
  He was convulsed.when he would speak your name,
  From such abysses of his heart it came.

XI

Now whether this be Weddah's self or not,
My Lady in her wisdom must decide.
The lady's questions ploughed the self-same spot
Over and over lest some grains should hide
Of this vast treasure fallen to her lot:
Swear by the Prophet's tomb I may confide
  In you as in myself until the end;
  And Om-el-Bonain lives and dies your friend.

XII

Brave Amine swore, and bravely held the vow.
Her mistress kept her babbling all that eve,
A pleasant rill. And on the morrow: Now
Go bid him tell all friends that he must leave
In seven days; so much we must allow,
So many starving hours of bliss bereave!
  His travels urge him in his own despite;
  He gives a farewell feast on such a night:

XIII

And in the meanwhile he shall fully learn
What is to follow. When this message came,
The thick dark in him 'gan to seethe and burn
Till soul and body fused in one clear flame.
His guests all blinked with wonder to discern
This glowing heart of joy; and flushed with shame
  Unmerited for having thought him cold,
  Who made their old feel young, their young feel old.

XIV

The long week passed; the morning came to crown
Or kill the lovers' hope. It was a day
Well chosen, for some guests of high renown
Left Walid, who would speed them on their way;
And festal tumult filled the sunny town.
The merchant in departure strolled astray
  Amongst the groups about the palace heaving
  To glimpse the rich procession form for leaving.

XV

And when it left, absorbing every eye;
A stream of splendours rolling with the din
Of horn and tabor under that blue sky;
Came Amine carelessly and led him in,
With chat of certain anklets she would buy;
And led him lounging onwards till they win
  A storeroom where her mistress daily spent
  Some matin hours on household cares intent.

XVI

Large chests were ranged around it, one of which
They had made ready with most loving care;
Lurked apertures among the carvings rich,
Above its deep soft couch, for light and air:
Behold your prison cell, your palace niche,
The jewel casket of my Lady fair!
  I lock you in; from her must come your key:
  Love's captives pay sweet ransom to get free!

XVII

She found her mistress fever-flushed, and told
Their full success: Our prisoner is secure;
A lion meek as lambkin of the fold,
Prepared your harshest torments to endure!
But, dearest Lady, as you have been bold,
Be prudent, prudent, prudent, and assure
  Long life to bliss. Now with your leave I go
  To be well seen of all the house below.

XVIII

She took another stairway for descent,
And sauntered round to the front courtyard gate,
Chatting and laughing lightly as she went
With various groups, all busy in debate
On those departed guests: and some were shent
For meanness maugre retinue and state,
  And some extolled for bounteous disposition,
  And all summed up with judgment-day precision.

XIX

Of all her fellow-slaves it seemed but one,
Whose breast was tinder for love's flame would she
Vouchsafe a spark, had spied the venture run:
Soho, my flirting madam, where is he
You brought in here an hour since with your fun?
A happy rogue, whoever he may be!
  Have you already tired of this new dandy,
  Or hid him somewhere to be always handy?

XX

The stupid jealous creature that you are!
Where were your eyes, then, not to know his face?
For weeks back he has dealt in our bazaar,
And now is on the road to some new place.
He had an emerald and diamond star
I thought might win my poor dear Lady's grace
  She would not even look at it, alack!
  I packed him off for ever with his pack.

XXI

Thus these long-hapless lovers for awhile,
Enringed with dreadful fire, safe ambush found,
Screened by its very glare; a magic isle
By roaring billows guarded well till drowned;
A refuge spot of green and liquid smile
Whose rampart was the simoon gathering round:
  If darkness hid them, it was thunder gloom
  Whose light must come in lightnings to consume

XXII

And even as Iskander's self, for whom
The whole broad earth sufficed not, found at last
Full scope vouchsafed him in the narrow tomb;
So he long pining in the desert vast
As in a dungeon, found now ample room,
Found perfect freedom and content, shut fast
  Alive within that coffer-coffin lonely,
  Which gave him issue to that chamber only.

XXIII

They knew what peril compassed them about,
But could not feel the dread it would inspire;
Imperious love shut other passions out,
Or made them fuel for his altar fire.
At first one sole thought harassed them with doubt;
To kill her lord and flee? Then tribe and sire
  Would justly curse them; for in every act
  He had been loyal to the evil pact.

XXIV

He had indeed wronged them; for well he knew
Their love from infancy, their plighted troth,
When merciless in mastery he drew
From her repugnant lips the fatal oath:
That love avenged the wrong of love was due;
But still his blood was sacred to them both;
  The tender husband and the proved ally
  They dare not harm; must death come, they could die.

XXV

Die! Often he would dream for hours supine
Upon his lidded couch, Life's dream is over;
I wait the resurrection in this shrine!
Anon an angel cometh to uncover
The inmost glories of the realm divine,
Because though dead I still am faithful lover
  My spirit drinks its fill of bliss, and then
  Sinks back into this twilight trance again.

XXVI

Like bird above its young one in the nest
Which cannot fly, he often heard her singing;
The thrill and swell of rapture from her breast
In fountains of delightful music springing:
It seemed he had been borne among the blest,
Whose quires around his darksome couch were ringing;
  Long after that celestial voice sank mute
  His heartstrings kept sweet tremble like a lute.

XXVII

She heard his breathing like a muffled chime,
She heard his tranquil heart-beats through the flow
Of busy menials in the morning time;
Far-couched at night she felt a sudden glow,
And straight her breathing answered rhyme for rhyme
His softest furtive footsteps to and fro:
  And none else heard? She marvelled how the sense
  Of living souls could be so dull and dense.

XXVIII

Once early, early, ere the dawn grew loud,
She stole to watch his slumber by its gleam;
And blushing with a soft laugh-gurgle bowed
And sank as in the bosom of a stream,
An ardent angel in a rosy cloud
Resolving the enchantment of his dream:
  Where there is room for thee, is room for us;
  So may I share thy death-sarcophagus!

XXIX

She grew so lovely, ravishing, and sweet,
Her brow so radiant and her lips so warm;
Such rich heart-music stirred her buoyant feet,
And swayed the gestures of her lithe young form,
And revelled in her voice to bliss complete;
That Walid whirled with his great passion's storm,
  Befooled with joy, went doting down his hell:
  Oh, tame and meek, my skittish wild gazelle!

XXX

Thus these, sings Hassan, of their love's full measure
Drank swiftly in that circle of swift fire;
A veil of light and ardour to their pleasure
Till it revealed their ashes on one pyre:
Some never win, some spend in youth this treasure,
And crawl down sad age starvelings of desire:
  These lavish royal wealth in one brief season,
  But death found both so rich he gave them reason.

PART IV.

I

The tender almond-blossom flushed and white
Sank floating in warm flakes through lucid air;
The rose flung forth into the sea of light
Her heart of fire and incense burning bare;
The nightingale thrilled all the breathless night
With passion so intense it seemed despair:
  And still these lovers drank love's perfect wine
  From that gold urn of secrecy divine.

II

Then Fate prepared the end. A grey old man,
Bowed down with grief who had not bent with time,
Made way to Walid in the full divan:
His son, great-hearted and in youth's hot prime,
Was now a fugitive and under ban
For an indignant deed of sinless crime;
  A noble heirloom pearl the suppliant brought
  To clear the clouded face ere he besought.

III

This pearl in Walid's mood of golden joy
Shone fair as morning star in rosy dawn;
He called his minion, Motar: Take this toy
Unto your Lady where she sits withdrawn,
With my love-greeting, and this message, boy:
Were this a string of such, a monarch's pawn,
  A pearl for every note, it would not pay
  That song I heard you singing yesterday.

IV

They had been leaning for an hour perchance,
Motionless, gazing in each other's eyes;
Floating in deep pure joy, whose still expanse
Rippled but rarely with long satiate sighs;
Their souls so intermingled in the trance,
So far away dissolved through fervent skies,
  That it was marvel how each fair mute form
  Without its pulse and breath remained life-warm.

V

When rapid footsteps almost at the door
Stung her to vigilance, and her fierce start
Shook Weddah, and that lion of proud war
Must flee to covert like a timid hart:
But drunken with the message he now bore
The saucy youth flew in, Fate's servile dart,
  Without announcement; and espied, what he,
  Still subtle though amazed, feigned not to see.

VI

The message with the goodly pearl he gave:
She could for wrath have ground it into dust
Between her richer teeth, and stabbed the slave
Who brought it; but most bitterly she must
Put on sweet smiles of pleasure, and the knave
With tender answer full of thanks entrust.
  He lingered: Our kind lady will bestow
    Some little mark of bounty ere I go?

VII

Her anger cried: Only the message dear
Has saved the messenger from punishment;
If evermore as now you enter here
You shall be scourged and starved and prison-pent.
He cowered away from her in sullen fear,
And darted from the room; and as he went
  The sting of her rebuke was curdling all
    His blood of vanity to poison gall.

VIII

He hissed in Walid's ear the seething spite:
My Lord's pearl by my Lady's was surpassed;
In that rich cedar coffer to the right
I saw the treasure being hidden fast;
A gallant, young and beautiful and bright.
Unmothered slave, be that foul lie your last!
  And clove the scandal with his instant sword
    Strong Walid: Motar had his full reward.

IX

When Weddah, plunged from glory into gloom,
Heard that last speech of Om-el-Bonain there
A sudden ominous sense of icy doom
Assailed his glowing heart with bleak despair.
The moment that false slave had left the room
She sprang to seize her lover in his lair:
  She bowed all quivering like a storm-swept palm;
  He rose to meet her solemn, pale and calm.

X

He clasped her with strong passion to his breast,
He kissed her with a very tender kiss:
Soul of my soul! what lives men call most blest
Can be compared to our brief lives in bliss?
But one wild year of anguish and unrest;
Three moons of perfect secret love! Were this
  My dying hour, I thankfully attest
  Of all earth's dooms I have enjoyed the best.

XI

What, weeping, thou, such kiss-unworthy tears!
The glory of the Azra must not weep,
Whom mighty Weddah worships, for cold fears;
But only for strong love, in stillness deep,
Secluded from all alien eyes and ears.
And now to vigil, and perchance to sleep,
  Enshrined once more: be proud and calm and strong;
  Your second visitor will come ere long.

XII

And scarcely was all said when Walid came,
Full gently stealing for a tiger-spring;
His love and fury, hope and fear and shame,
All mad with venom from that serpent's sting,
Like wild beasts huddled in a den of flame
Within the cool white palace of a king:
  She rose to greet; he deigned no glance of quest,
  But went and lolled upon that cedar chest

XIII

I come like any haggler of the mart,
Who having sent a bauble seeks its price:
Will you forgive the meanness of my part,
And one of these fair coffers sacrifice?
A clutch of iron fingers gript her heart
Till it seemed bursting in the cruel vice:
  And yet she quivered not, nor breathed a moan:
  Are not myself and all things here your own?

XIV

I thank you for the bountiful award;
And choose, say this whereon I now sit here?
Take any, take them all; but that, my Lord,
Is full of household stuff and woman's gear.
I want the coffer, not what it may hoard,
However rich and beautiful and dear.
  And it is thine, she said; and this the key:
  Her royal hand outheld it steadfastly.

XV

Swift as a double flash from thunder-skies
The angel and the devil of his doubt
Flamed from the sombre windows of his eyes:
He went and took the key she thus held out,
And turned as if he would unlock his prize.
She breathed not; all the air ran blood about
  A swirl of terrors and wild hopes of guilt;
  Calm Weddah seized, then loosed, his dagger-hilt.

XVI

But Walid had restrained himself, and thought:
Shall I unlock the secret of my soul,
The mystery of my Fate, that has been brought
So perfectly within my own control?
That were indeed a work by folly wrought:
For Time, in this my vassal, must unroll
  To me, and none but me, what I would learn;
  I hold the vantage, undiscerned discern.

XVII

He summoned certain slaves, and bade them bear
The coffer he had sealed with his own seal
Into a room below with strictest care;
And followed thoughtful at the last one's heel.
At noontide Amine found her mistress there,
Benumbed with horror, deaf to her appeal;
  The sightless eyes fixed glaring on that door
  By which her soul had vanished evermore.

XVIII

Beneath the cedar whose noonshadow large,
Level from massive trunk, outspread halfway
Adown a swardslope to the river marge,
Where rosebowers shone between the willows grey,
The wondering bearers bore their heavy charge;
And where the central shadow thickest lay
  He bade them delve a pit, and delve it deep
  Till watersprings against their strokes should leap.

XIX

Then waved them to a distance, while he bowed
Upon the coffer, harkening for a space:
If truth bought that poor wretch his bloody shroud,
I bury thus her guilt and my disgrace;
And you, as by the whole earth disavowed,
Sink into nothingness and leave no trace .
  If not, it is a harmless whim enough
  To sepulchre a chest of household stuff.

XX

With face encircled by his hands, which leaned
Upon the wood, he challenged clear and slow:
The hollow sound, his full hot breath thus screened
Suffused his visage with a tingling glow;
His pulse, his vesture's rustling intervened
And marred the silence: he drew back, and so
  Knelt listening yet awhile with bated breath:
  The secret lay as mute and still as death.

XXI

Above there in her chamber Weddah might
Have leapt forth suddenly their foe to kill.
Ev'n here with hazard of swift fight and flight
Escaped or perished as a warrior still:
But thus through him her name had suffered blight:
He locked his breath and nerves with rigid will.
  So Walid first let sink his key unused,
   Then signed the slaves back: they wrought on, he mused.

XXII

Against the dark bulk swelled the waters thin,
The stones and earth were trampled to a mound
He then broke silence stern and sad: Within
That coffer ye have buried, sealed and bound,
Lies one of the most potent evil djinn,
Whose hate on me and mine hath darkly frowned;
  He sought to kill your mistress: Hell and Doom
   And Allah's curse all guard this dungeon tomb!

XXIII

And Walid never spoke of this again,
And none dared ask him; for his brow grew black,
His eye flamed evil and appalling when
Some careless word but strayed upon a track
That might from far lead to it: therefore men
Spoke only of the thing behind his back.
  The cedar shadow centred by that mound
   Was sacredly eschewed as haunted ground.

XXIV

But one pale phantom, noon and night and morn,
Was ever seen there; quiet as a stone,
Huddled and shapeless, weeping tears forlorn
As silent as the dews; her heart alone
And not her lips, whose seal was never torn,
Upbraiding sluggish death with constant moan.
  Hushed whispers circled, piteous eyes were wet;
  The captive djinnee holds her captive yet.

XXV

Thus Walid learned too well the bitter truth,
His home dissolved, its marvellous joy a cheat;
Yet gave no sign to her: for there was ruth
Of memories gall itself left subtly sweet;
And consciousness of wrong against her youth,
And surfeit of a vengeance so complete:
  He could not stab her bleeding heart; her name
  With his own honour he kept pure from shame.

XXVI

She thought Death dead, or prisoned in deep Hell
As sole assuager of the human lot:
But when the evening of the seventh day fell
Walid alone dared tread the fatal spot:
She crouched as who would plunge into a well,
Livid and writhed into a desperate knot;
  Her fingers clutched like talons in the mould:
  Thus the last time his arms about her fold.

XXVII

As if to glut the demon with her doom,
And break the spell, there where her corse was found
He had it buried; and a simple tomb
Of black-domed marble sealed the dolorous mound;
And there was set to guard the cedar gloom
A triple cirque of cypress-trees around:
  Thus Love wrought Destiny to join his slaves
  Weddah and Om-el-Bonain in their graves.

XXVIII

True Amine, freed and richly dowered, no less
Had served until the end her lady dear;
And shrouded for the grave that loveliness
Whose noon-eclipse left life without its peer:
Then sought the Azra in her lone distress,
And tended Abd-el-Aziz through the sere
  Forlorn last days; and married in the clan,
  And bore brave children to a valiant man.

XXIX

Great Walid lived long years beyond this woe,
And still increased in wealth and power and glory;
A loyal friend, a formidable foe;
Each Azra was his mother's child saith story;
And he saw goodly children round him grow
To keep his name green when Death took him hoary:
  So prosperous, was he happy too? the sage
  Cites this one counsel of his reverend age:

XXX

Have brood-mares in your stables, my young friend,
And women in your harem, but no wife:
A common daggerblade may pierce or rend,
A month bring healing; this, the choicest knife
In Fate's whole armoury, wounds beyond amend,
And with a scratch can poison all your life:
  And it lies naked in your naked breast
  When you are drunk with joy and sleep's rich rest

XXXI

As surely as a very precious stone
Finds out that jeweller who doth excel,
So surely to the bard becometh known
The tale which only he can fitly tell:
A few years thence, and Walid's heart alone
Had thrilled not to a talisman's great spell,
  His deathstone set in Hassan's golden verse;
  Here poorly copied in cheap bronze or worse.

XXXII

He ends: We know not which to most admire;
The lover who went silent to his doom;
The spouse obedient to her lord's just ire,
The mistress faithful to her lover's tomb;
The husband calm in jealousy's fierce fire,
Who strode unswerving through the doubtful gloom
  To vengeance instant, secret and complete,
  And did not strike one blow more than was meet.

XXXIII

With stringent cords of circumstance dark Fate
Doth certain lives here so entoil and mesh
That some or all must strangle if they wait,
And knife to cut the knots must cut quick flesh:
The first strong arm free severs ere too late;
Fresh writhings would but tangle it afresh:
  To die with valiant fortitude, to kill
    As priest not butcher; so much scope has will.

XXXIV

These perished, and he slew them in such wise
That all may meet as friends and free from shame,
Whether they meet in Hell or Paradise,
If he has won long life and power and fame,
Our darlings too have won their own set prize,
Conjoined for evermore in true love's name:
  The Azra die when they do love, of old
    Was graven with the iron pen, on gold.

XXXV

May Allah grant eternal joy and youth
In fateless Heaven to one and all of these.
And for himself a little grain of ruth
The bard will beg, this once, while on his knees;
Who cannot always see the very truth,
And does not always sing the truth he sees,
  But something pleasanter to foolish ears
    That should be tickled not with straws but spears.

Sunday Up The River

AN IDYLL OF COCKAIGNE.

En allant promener aux champs,
J'y ai trouvé les blés si grands,
Les aubépiries florissant.
  En vérité, en vérité,
C'est le mois, le joli mois,
C'est le joli mois de mai

…

'Dieu veuill' garder les vins, les blés,
Les jeunes filles à marier,
Les jeun' garçons pour les aimer!
  En vérité, en vérité,
C'est le mois, le joli mois,
C'est le joli mois de mai.

Carol of Lorraine
from Victor Fournel's charming book,
'Ce qu'on voit dans les rues de Paris.'

I

I looked out into the morning,
 I looked out into the west:
The soft blue eye of the quiet sky
 Still drooped in dreamy rest;

The trees were still like clouds there,
 The clouds like mountains dim;
The broad mist lay, a silver bay
 Whose tide was at the brim.

I looked out into the morning,
  I looked out into the east:
The flood of light upon the night
  Had silently increased;

The sky was pale with fervour,
  The distant trees were grey,
The hill-lines drawn like waves of dawn
  Dissolving in the day.

I looked out into the morning;
  Looked east, looked west, with glee:
O richest day of happy May,
  My love will spend with me!

II

'Oh, what are you waiting for here, young man?
  What are you looking for over the bridge?'
A little straw hat with the streaming blue ribbons
  Is soon to come dancing over the bridge.

Her heart beats the measure that keeps her feet dancing,
  Dancing along like a wave o'the sea;
Her heart pours the sunshine with which her eyes glancing
  Light up strange faces in looking for me.

The strange faces brighten in meeting her glances;
  The strangers all bless her, pure, lovely, and free:
She fancies she walks, but her walk skips and dances,
  Her heart makes such music in coming to me.

Oh, thousands and thousands of happy young maidens
  Are tripping this morning their sweethearts to see;

But none whose heart beats to a sweeter love-cadence
  Than hers who will brighten the sunshine for me.

'Oh, what are you waiting for here, young man?
  What are you looking for over the bridge?'
  A little straw hat with the streaming blue ribbons;
  —And here it comes dancing over the bridge!

III

      In the vast vague grey,
Mistily luminous, brightly dim,
The trees to the south there, far away,
Float as beautiful, strange and grand
As pencilled palm-trees every line
Mystic with a grace divine,
In our dreams of the holy Eastern Land.

There is not a cloud in the sky;
      The vague vast grey
Melts into azure dim on high.
Warmth, and languor, and infinite peace!
      Surely the young Day
Hath fallen into a vision and a trance,
And his burning flight doth cease.

      Yet look how here and there
Soft curves, fine contours, seem to swim,
Half emerging, wan and dim,
      Into the quiet air:
Like statues growing slowly, slowly out
From the great vault of marble; here a limb,
And there a feature, but the rest all doubt.

Then the sculpturing sunbeams smite,
  And the forms start forth to the day;
And the breath of the morning sweepeth light
  The luminous dust away:
    And soon, soon, soon,
Crowning the floor of the land and the sea,
  Shall be wrought the dome of Noon.

  The burning sapphire dome,
With solemn imagery; vast shapes that stand
Each like an island ringed with flashing foam,
Black-purple mountains, creeks and rivers of light,
Crags of cleft crystal blazing to the crest:
  Vast isles that move, that roam
A tideless sea of infinite fathomless rest.

    Thus shall it be this noon:
And thus, so slowly, slowly from its birth
    In the long night's dark swoon,
Through the long morning's trance, sweet, vague, and dim,
    The Sun divine above
Doth build up in us, Heaven completing Earth,
    Our solemn Noon of Love.

IV

The church bells are ringing:
  How green the earth, how fresh and fair!
The thrushes are singing:
  What rapture but to breathe this air!

The church bells are ringing:
  Lo, how the river dreameth there!
The thrushes are singing:
  Green flames wave lightly everywhere!

The church bells are ringing:
  How all the world breathes praise and prayer!
The thrushes are singing:
  What Sabbath peace doth trance the air!

V

I love all hardy exercise
  That makes one strain and quiver;
And best of all I love and prize
  This boating on our river.
    I to row and you to steer,
    Gay shall be Life's trip, my dear:
    You to steer and I to row,
    All is bright where'er we go.

We push off from the bank; again
  We're free upon the waters;
The happiest of the sons of men,
  The fairest of earth's daughters.
    And I row, and I row;
    The blue floats above us as we go:
    And you steer, and you steer,
    Framed in gliding wood and water, O my dear.

I pull a long calm mile or two,
  Pull slowly, deftly feather:
How sinful *any* work to do
  In this Italian weather!
    Yet I row, yet I row;
    The blue floats above us as we go:
    While you steer, while you steer,
    Framed in gliding wood and water, O my dear.

Those lovely breadths of lawn that sweep
  Adown in still green billows!
And o'er the brim in fountains leap;
  Green fountains, weeping willows!
    And I row, and I row;
    The blue floats above us as we go:
    And you steer, and you steer,
Framed in gliding wood and water, O my dear.

We push among the flags in flower,
  Beneath the branches tender,
And we are in a faerie bower
  Of green and golden splendour.
    I to row and you to steer,
    Gay must be Life's trip, my dear;
    You to steer and I to row,
    All is bright where'er we go.

A secret bower where we can hide
  In lustrous shadow lonely;
The crystal floor may lap and glide
  To rock our dreaming only
    I to row and you to steer,
    Gay must be Life's trip, my dear;
    You to steer and I to row,
    All is bright where'er we go.

VI

I love this hardy exercise,
  This strenuous toil of boating:
Our skiff beneath the willow lies
  Half stranded and half floating.

As I lie, as I lie,
Glimpses dazzle of the blue and burning sky;
As you lean, as you lean,
Faerie Princess of the secret faerie scene.

My shirt is of the soft red wool,
  My cap is azure braided
By two white hands so beautiful,
  My tie mauve purple-shaded.
    As I lie, as I lie,
    Glimpses dazzle of white clouds and sapphire sky
    As you lean, as you lean,
    Faerie Princess of the secret faerie scene.

Your hat with long blue streamers decked,
  Your pure throat crimson-banded;
White-robed, my own white dove unflecked,
  Dove-footed, lilac handed.
    As I lie, as I lie,
    Glimpses dazzle of white clouds and sapphire sky;
    As you lean, as you lean,
    Faerie Princess of the secret faerie scene.

If any boaters boating past
  Should look where we're reclining,
They'll say, To-day green willows glassed
  Rubies and sapphires shining!
    As I lie, as I lie,
    Glimpses dazzle of the blue and burning sky;
    As you lean, as you lean,
    Faerie Princess of the secret faerie scene.

VII

Grey clouds come purring from my lips,
  And hang there softly curling,
While from the bowl now leaps, now slips,
  A steel-blue thread high twirling.
    As I lie, as I lie,
    The hours fold their wings beneath the sky;
    As you lean, as you lean,
    In that trance of perfect love and bliss serene.

I gaze on you and I am crowned,
  A monarch great and glorious,
A Hero in all realms renowned,
  A Faerie Prince victorious.
    As I lie, as I lie,
    The hours fold their wings beneath the sky;
    As you lean, as you lean,
    In that trance of perfect love and bliss serene.

Your violet eyes pour out their whole
  Pure light in earnest rapture;
Your thoughts come dreaming through my soul,
  And nestle past recapture.
    As I lie, as I lie,
    The hours fold their wings beneath the sky;
    As you lean, as you lean,
    In that trance of perfect love and bliss serene.

O friends, your best years to the oar
  Like galley-slaves devoting,
This is and shall be evermore
  The true sublime of boating!
    As I lie, as I lie,

The hours fold their wings beneath the sky;
As you lean, as you lean,
In that trance of perfect love and bliss serene.

VIII

The water is cool and sweet and pure,
  The water is clear as crystal;
And water's a noble liquid, sure;—
  But look at my pocket-pistol!

Tim Boyland gave it me, one of two
  The rogue brought back from Dublin:
With a jar of the genuine stuff: hurroo!
  How deliciously it comes bubblin'!

It is not brandy, it is not wine,
  It is Jameson's Irish Whisky:
It fills the heart with joy divine,
  And it makes the fancy frisky.

All other spirits are vile resorts,
  Except its own Scotch first cousin;
And as for your Clarets and Sherries and Ports,
  A naggin is worth a dozen.

I have watered this, though a toothful neat
  Just melts like cream down the throttle:
But it's grand in the punch, hot, strong, and sweet!
  Not a headache in a bottle.

It is amber as the western skies
  When the sunset glows serenest;
It is mellow as the mild moonrise
When the shamrock leaves fold greenest.

Just a little, wee, wee, tiny sip!
  Just the wet of the bill of a starling!
A drop of dew for the rosy lip,
  And two stars in the eyes of my darling!

'Faith your kiss has made it so sweet at the brim
  I could go on supping for ever!
We'll pocket the pistol: And Tim, you limb,
  May this *craturr* abandon you never!

IX

Like violets pale i' the Spring o' the year
  Came my Love's sad eyes to my youth;
Wan and dim with many a tear,
  But the sweeter for that in sooth:
        Wet and dim,
        Tender and true,
        Violet eyes
      Of the sweetest blue.

Like pansies dark i'the June o'the year
  Grow my Love's glad eyes to my prime;
Rich with the purple splendour clear
  Of their thoughtful bliss sublime:
        Deep and dark,
        Solemn and true,
        Pansy eyes
      Of the noblest blue

X

Were I a real Poet, I would sing
Such joyous songs of you, and all mere truth;
As true as buds and tender leaves in Spring,
As true as lofty dreams in dreamful youth;
That men should cry: How foolish every one
Who thinks the world is getting out of tune!
Where is the tarnish in our golden sun?
Where is the clouding in our crystal moon?
The lark sings now the eversame new song
With which it soared through Eden's purest skies;
This poet's music doth for us prolong
The very speech Love learnt in Paradise;
This maiden is as young and pure and fair
As Eve agaze on Adam sleeping there.

XI

When will you have not a sole kiss left,
And my prodigal mouth be all bereft?
  When your lips have ravished the last sweet flush
  Of the red with which the roses blush:
  Now I kiss them and kiss them till they hush.

When will you have not a glance to give
Of the love in whose lustre my glances live?
  When, O my darling, your fathomless eyes
  Have drawn all the azure out of the skies:
  Now I gaze and I gaze till they dare not rise.

When will you find not a single vow
Of the myriads and myriads you lavish now?
  When your voice has gurgled the last sweet note

That was meant from the nightingales to float:
Now I whisper it, whisper it dumb in your throat.

When will you love me no more, no more,
And my happy, happy dream be o'er?
  When no rose is red, and no skies are blue,
  And no nightingale sings the whole year through,
  Then my heart may have no love for you.

XII

My Love o'er the water bends dreaming;
  It glideth and glideth away:
She sees there her own beauty, gleaming
  Through shadow and ripple and spray.

Oh, tell her, thou murmuring river,
  As past her your light wavelets roll,
How steadfast that image for ever
  Shines pure in pure depths of my soul.

XIII

The wandering airs float over the lawn,
And linger and whisper in at our bovver;
    (They babble, babble all they know:)
The delicate secrets they have drawn
From bird and meadow and tree and flower;
    (Gossiping softly, whispering low.)

Some linden stretches itself to the height,
Then rustles back to its dream of the day;
    (They babble, babble all they know:)
Some bird would trill out its love-delight,

But the honey melts in its throat away;
    (Gossiping softly, whispering low.)

Some flower seduced by the treacherous calm
Breathes all its soul in a fragrant sigh;
    (They babble, babble all they know:)
Some blossom weeps a tear of balm
For the lost caress of a butterfly;
    (Gossiping softly, whispering low.)

Our Mother lies in siesta now,
And we listen to her breathings here;
    (They babble, babble all they know:)
And we learn all the thoughts hid under her brow,
All her heart's deep dreams of the happy year:
    (Gossiping softly, whispering low.)

XIV

Those azure, azure eyes
    Gaze on me with their love;
And I am lost in dream,
    And cannot speak or move.

Those azure, azure eyes
    Stay with me when we part;
A sea of azure thoughts
    Overfloods my heart.*

XV

Give a man a horse he can ride,
    Give a man a boat he can sail;
And his rank and wealth, his strength and health,
    On sea nor shore shall fail.

Give a man a pipe he can smoke,
  Give a man a book he can read;
And his home is bright with a calm delight,
  Though the room be poor indeed.

Give a man a girl he can love,
  As I, O my love, love thee;
And his heart is great with the pulse of Fate,
  At home, on land, on sea.

XVI

My love is the flaming Sword
    To fight through the world;
Thy love is the Shield to ward,
And the Armour of the Lord,
    And the Banner of Heaven unfurled.

XVII

Let my voice ring out and over the earth,
    Through all the grief and strife,
With a golden joy in a silver mirth:
        Thank God for Life!

Let my voice swell out through the great abyss
    To the azure dome above,
With a chord of faith in the harp of bliss:
        Thank God for Love!

Let my voice thrill out beneath and above
    The whole world through:
O my Love and Life, O my Life and Love,
        Thank God for you!

XVIII

The wine of Love is music,
    And the feast of Love is song:
And when Love sits down to the banquet,
    Love sits long:

Sits long and ariseth drunken,
    But not with the feast and the wine;
He reeleth with his own heart,
    That great rich Vine.

XIX

Drink! drink! open your mouth!
    This air is as rich as wine;
Flowing with balm from the sunny south,
    And health from the western brine.

Drink! drink! open your mouth!
    This air is as strong as wine:
My brain is drugged with the balm o'the south,
    And rolls with the western brine.

Drink! drink! open your mouth!
    This air is the choicest wine;
From that golden grape the Sun, i'the south
    Of Heaven's broad vine.

XX

    Could we float thus ever,
    Floating down a river,
Down a tranquil river, and you alone with me:

Past broad shining meadows,
Past the great wood-shadows,
Past fair farms and hamlets, for ever to the sea.

Through the golden noonlight,
Through the silver moonlight,
Through the tender gloaming, gliding calm and free;
From the sunset gliding,
Into morning sliding,
With the tranquil river for ever to the sea.

Past the masses hoary
Of cities great in story,
Past their towers and temples drifting lone and free:
Gliding, never hasting,
Gliding, never resting,
Ever with the river that glideth to the sea.

With a swifter motion
Out upon the Ocean,
Heaven above and round us, and you alone with me:
Heaven around and o'er us,
The Infinite before us,
Floating on for ever upon the flowing sea.

.   .   .   .   .

What time is it, dear, now?
We are in the year now
Of the New Creation one million two or three.
But where are we now, Love?
We are as I trow, Love,
In the Heaven of Heavens upon the Crystal Sea.

And may mortal sinners
Care for carnal dinners
In your Heaven of Heavens, New Era millions three?
Oh, if their boat gets stranding
Upon some Richmond landing,
They're thirsty as the desert and hungry as the sea!

*'Mit deinen blauen Augen
    Siehst du mich lieblich an;
Da ward mir so traumend zu Sinne
    Dass ich nicht sprechen kann.

'An deine blauen Augen
    Gedenk' ich allerwärts; —
Ein Meer von blauen Gedanken
    Ergiesst sich über mein Herz.'

—Heine

Sunday At Hampstead

AN IDLE IDYLL BY A VERY HUMBLE MEMBER OF
THE GREAT AND NOBLE LONDON MOB.

I

This is the Heath of Hampstead,
There is the dome of Saint Paul's
Beneath, on the serried house-tops,
A chequered lustre falls:

And the mighty city of London,
Under the clouds and the light,
Seems a low wet beach, half shingle,
With a few sharp rocks upright.

Here will we sit, my darling,
And dream an hour away:
The donkeys are hurried and worried,
But we are not donkeys to-day:

Through all the weary week, dear,
We toil in the murk down there,
Tied to a desk and a counter,
A patient stupid pair!

But on Sunday we slip our tether,
And away from the smoke and the smirch;
Too grateful to God for His Sabbath
To shut its hours in a church.

Away to the green, green country,
Under the open sky;

Where the earth's sweet breath is incense
And the lark sings psalms on high.

On Sunday we're Lord and Lady,
With ten times the love and glee
Of those pale and languid rich ones
Who are always and never free.

They drawl and stare and simper,
So fine and cold and staid,
Like exquisite waxwork figures
That must be kept in the shade:

We can laugh out loud when merry,
We can romp at kiss-in-the-ring,
We can take our beer at a public,
We can loll on the grass and sing. . . .

Would you grieve very much, my darling,
If all yon low wet shore
Were drowned by a mighty flood-tide,
And we never toiled there more?

Wicked? —there is no sin, dear,
In an idle dreamer's head;
He turns the world topsy-turvy
To prove that his soul's not dead.

I am sinking, sinking, sinking;
It is hard to sit upright!
Your lap is the softest pillow!
Good-night, my Love, good night!

II

How your eyes dazzle down into my soul!
  I drink and drink of their deep violet wine,
And ever thirst the more, although my whole
  Dazed being whirls in drunkenness divine.

Pout down your lips from that bewildering smile,
  And kiss me for the interruption, Sweet!
I had escaped you: floating for awhile
  In that far cloud ablaze with living heat:

I floated with it through the solemn skies,
  I melted with it up the Crystal Sea
Into the Heaven of Heavens; and shut my eyes
  To feel eternal rest enfolding me. . . .

Well, I prefer one tyrannous girl down here,
  You jealous violet-eyed Bewitcher, you!
To being lord in Mohammed's seventh sphere
  Of meekest houris threescore ten and two!

III

Was it hundreds of years ago, my Love,
  Was it thousands of miles away,
That two poor creatures we know, my Love,
  Were toiling day by day;
        Were toiling weary, weary,
        With many myriads more,
        In a City dark and dreary
        On a sullen river's shore?

Was it truly a fact or a dream, my Love?
  I think my brain still reels,
And my ears still throbbing seem, my Love,
  With the rush and the clang of wheels;
        Of a vast machinery roaring
        For ever in skyless gloom;
        Where the poor slaves peace imploring
        Found peace alone in the tomb.

Was it hundreds of years ago, my Love,
  Was it thousands of miles away?
Or was it a dream to show, my Love,
  The rapture of to-day?
        This day of holy splendour,
        This Sabbath of rich rest,
        Wherein to God we render
        All praise by being blest.

IV

Eight of us promised to meet here
And tea together at five:
And —who would ever believe it?—
We are the first to arrive!

Oh, shame on us, my darling;
It is a monstrous crime
To make a tryst with *others*
And be before our time!

Lizzie is off with William,
Quite happy for her part;
Our sugar in her pocket,
And the sweet love in her heart.

Mary and Dick so grandly
Parade suburban streets;
His waistcoat and her bonnet
Proving the best of treats.

And Fanny plagues big Robert
With tricks of the wildest glee:
O Fanny, *you'll* get in hot water
If you do not bring us our tea!

Why, bless me, look at that table,
Every one of them there!—
'Ha, here at last we have them,
The always behindhand pair!'

'When the last trumpet-solo
Strikes up instead of the lark,
They'll turn in their sleep just grunting
Who's up so soon in the dark? '

Babble and gabble, you rabble,
A thousand in full yell!
And this is your Tower of Babel,
This not-to-be-finished Hotel.*

'You should see it in the drawing,
You'd think a Palace they make,
Like the one in the *Lady of Lyons*,
With this pond for the lovely lake!'

'I wish it wasn't Sunday,
There's no amusement at all:
Who was here Hot-cross-bun-day?
We had such an open-air ball!

'The bands played polkas, waltzes,
Quadrilles; it was glorious fun!
And each gentleman gave them a penny
After each dance was done.'

'Mary is going to chapel,
And what takes her there, do you guess?
Her sweet little duck of a bonnet,
And her new second-hand silk dress.'

'*We* went to Church one Sunday,
But felt we had no right there;
For it's only a place for the grand folk
Who come in a carriage and pair.

'And I laughed out loud, - it was shameful!
But Fanny said, *Oh, what lives !*
He must have been clever, the rascal,
To manage seven hundred wives!'

'Suppose we play Hunt-the-Slipper?'
'We can't, there's the crinoline!'— 'Phew!
Bother it, always a nuisance!'
'Hoop-de-dooden-do!'

'I think I've seen all the girls here,
About a thousand, or more;
But none of them half so pretty
As our own loving four.'

'*Thank* you! and I've been listening
To lots of the men, the knaves;
But none of them half such humbugs
As our devoted slaves.'

'Do you see those purple flushes?
The sun will set in state:
Up all! we must cross to the heath, friends,
Before it gets too late.

'We will couch in the fern together,
And watch for the moon and the stars;
And the slim tree-tops will be lighted,
So the boys may light their cigars.

'And while the sunset glory
Burns down in crimson and gold,
LAZY shall tell us a story
Of his wonderful times of old.'

V.

Ten thousand years ago, ('*No more than that?*')
Ten thousand years, ('*The age of Robert's hat!*' —
'*Silence, you gods!* —'*Pinch Fanny!* — '*Now we're good.*')
This place where we are sitting was a wood,
Savage and desert save for one rude home
Of wattles plastered with stiff clay and loam;
And here, in front, upon the grassy mire
Four naked squaws were squatted round a fire:
Then four tall naked wild men crushing through
The tangled underwood came into view;
Two of them bent beneath a mighty boar,
The third was gashed and bleeding, number four
Strutted full-drest in war-paint, ('*That was Dick!*')
Blue of a devilish pattern laid on thick.
The squaws jumped up to roast the carcass whole;
The braves sank silent, stark 'gainst root and bole.
The meat half-done, they tore it and devoured,

Sullenly ravenous; the women cowered
Until their lords had finished, then partook.
Mist rose; all crept into their cabin-nook,
And staked the mouth; the floor was one broad bed
Of rushes dried with fox and bearskins spread.
Wolves howled and wild cats wailed; they snored; and so
The long night passed, shedding a storm of snow;
This very night ten thousand years ago.

VI

Ten thousand years before, ('*Come, draw it mild!*
Don't waste Conk-ology like that, my child!')
From where we sit to the horizon's bound
A level brilliant plain was spread all round,
As level and as brilliant as a sea
Under the burning sun; high as your knee
Aflame with flowers, yellow and blue and red:
Long lines of palm-trees marked out there the bed
Of a great river, and among them gleamed
A few grey tents. Then four swift horsemen streamed
Out of the West, magnificent in ire,
Churning the meadow into flakes of fire,
Brandishing monstrous spears as if in fight,
They wheeled, ducked, charged, and shouted fierce delight:
So till they reach the camp: the women there
Awaiting them the evening meal prepare;
Milk from the goats and camels, dates plucked fresh,
Cool curds and cheese, millet, sweet broiled kid's flesh.
The spear struck deep hath picketed each barb;
A grave proud turbaned man in flowing garb
Sups with a grave meek woman, humbly proud,
Whose eyes flash empire. Then the solemn crowd
Of stars above, the silent plain below,

Until the East resumes its furnace-glow;
This same night twenty thousand years ago.

VII

Ten thousand years before, ('*But if you take
Such mouthfuls, you will soon eat up Time's cake!*')
Where we are sitting rose in splendid light
A broad cool marble palace; from the height
Broad terrace-gardens stairlike sank away
Down to the floor of a deep sapphire bay.
Where the last slope slid greenly to the wave,
And dark rich glossy foliage shadow gave,
Four women —or four goddesses—leaned calm,
Of mighty stature, graceful as the palm:
One stroked with careless hand a lion's rnane,
One fed an eagle; while a measured strain
Was poured forth by the others, harp and voice,
Music to make the universe rejoice.
An isle was in the offing seen afar,
Deep-purple based, its peak a glittering star;
Whence rowed a galley (drooped the silken sails),
A dragon-barque with golden burning scales.
Then four bronzed giants leapt to land, embraced
The glorious women chanting: 'Did we haste?
The Cavern-Voice hath silenced all your fears;
Peace on our earth another thousand years!'
On fruits and noble wine, with song's rich flow,
They feasted in the sunset's golden glow;
This same night thirty thousand years ago.

VIII

Ten thousand years before, (*'Another ten!*
Good Lord, how greedy are these little men!')
This place where we are sitting (*'Half asleep.'*)
Was in the sea a hundred fathoms deep:
A floor of silver sand so fine and soft,
A coral forest branching far aloft;
Above, the great dusk emerald golden-green;
Silence profound and solitude serene.
Four mermaids sit beneath the coral rocks,
Combing with golden combs their long green locks,
And wreathing them with little pearly shells;
Four mermen come from out the deep-sea dells,
And whisper to them, and they all turn pale:
Then through the hyaline a voice of wail,
With passionate gestures, 'Ever alas for woe!'
A rumour cometh down the Ocean-flow,
A word calamitous! that we shall be
All disinherited from the great sea:
Our tail with which like fishes we can swim
Shall split into an awkward double-limb,
And we must waddle on the arid soil,
And build dirt-huts, and get our food with toil,
And lose our happy, happy lives! 'And so
These gentle creatures wept 'Alas for woe!'
This same night forty thousand years ago.

IX

'Are you not going back a little more?
What was the case ten thousand years before?'
Ten thousand years before 'twas Sunday night;
Four lovely girls were listening with delight,

Three noble youths admired another youth
Discoursing History crammed full of truth:
They all were sitting upon Hampstead Heath,
And monstrous grimy London lay beneath.
'The stupidest story LAZY ever told;
I've no more faith in his fine times of old.'
'How do you like our prospects now, my dears?
We'll all be mermaids in ten thousand years.'
'Mermaids are beautiful enough, but law!
Think of becoming a poor naked squaw!'
'But in these changes, sex will change no doubt;
We'll all be men and women turn about.'
'Then these four chaps will be the squaws? — that's just;
With lots of picaninnies, I *do* trust!'
'If changes go by fifty thousand, yes;
But if by ten, they last were squaws, I guess!'
'Come on; we'll go and do the very beers
We did this night was fifty thousand years.'
Thou prophet, thou deep sage! we'll go, we'll go:
The ring is round, Life naught, the World an O;
This night is fifty thousand years ago!

X

As we rush, as we rush in the Train,
    The trees and the houses go wheeling back,
But the starry heavens above the plain
    Come flying on our track.

All the beautiful stars of the sky,
    The silver doves of the forest of Night,
Over the dull earth swarm and fly,
    Companions of our flight.

We will rush ever on without fear;
  Let the goal be far, the flight be fleet!
For we carry the Heavens with us, Dear,
  While the Earth slips from our feet!

XI

Day after day of this azure May
The blood of the Spring has swelled in my veins;
Night after night of broad moonlight
A mystical dream has dazzled my brains.

A seething might, a fierce delight,
The blood of the Spring is the wine of the world
My veins run fire and thrill desire,
Every leaf of my heart's red rose uncurled.

A sad sweet calm, a tearful balm,
The light of the Moon is the trance of the world;
My brain is fraught with yearning thought,
And the rose is pale and its leaves are furled.

O speed the day, thou dear, dear May,
And hasten the night I charge thee, O June,
When the trance divine shall burn with the wine
And the red rose unfurl all its fire to the Moon!

XII

    O mellow moonlight warm,
    Weave round my Love a charm;
    O countless starry eyes,
    Watch from the holy skies;
    O ever-solemn Night,

Shield her within thy might:
 Watch her, my little one!
 Shield her, my darling!

How my heart shrinks with fear,
Nightly to leave thee, dear;
Lonely and pure within
Vast glooms of woe and sin:
Our wealth of love and bliss
Too heavenly-perfect is:
 Good night, my little one!
 God keep thee, darling!

*Since finished, in a fashion. The verses were written in 1863.

He Heard Her Sing

We were now in the midmost Maytime, in the full green
    flood of the Spring,
When the air is sweet all the daytime with the blossoms
    and birds that sing;
When the air is rich all the night, and richest of all in
    its noon;
When the nightingales pant the delight and keen stress
    of their love to the moon;
When the almond and apple and pear spread wavering
    wavelets of snow
In the light of the soft warm air far-flushed with a delicate
    glow;
When the towering chestnuts uphold their masses of
    spires red or white,
And the pendulous tresses of gold of the slim laburnum
    burn bright,
And the lilac guardeth the bowers with the gleam of a
    lifted spear,
And the scent of the hawthorn flowers breathes all the
    new life of the year,
And the linden's tender pink bud by the green of the
    leaf is o'errun,
And the bronze-beech shines like blood in the light of
    the morning sun,
And the leaf-buds seem spangling some network of
    gossamer flung on the elm,
And the hedges are filling their fretwork with every
    sweet green of Spring's realm;
And the flowers are everywhere budding and blowing
    about our feet,
The green of the meadows star-studding and the
    bright green blades of the wheat.

An evening and night of song. For first when I left
    the town,
And took the lane that is long and came out on the
    breeze-swept down,
The sunset heavens were all ringing wide over the golden
    gorse
With the skylarks' rapturous singing, a revel of larks
    in full force,
A revel of larks in the raptures surpassing all raptures of
    Man,
Who ponders the blessings he captures and finds in each
    blessing some ban.
And then I went on down the dale in the light of the
    afterglow,
In that strange light green and pale and serene and
    pathetic and slow
In its fading round to the north, while the light of the
    unseen moon
From the east comes brightening forth an ever-increasing
    boon.
And there in the cottage my Alice, through the hours so
    short and so long,
Kept filled to the brim love's chalice with the wine of
    music and song:
And first with colossal Beethoven, the gentlest spirit
    sublime
Of the harmonies interwoven, Eternity woven with Time;
Of the melodies slowly and slowly dissolving away through
    the soul,
While it dissolves with them wholly and our being is
    lost in the Whole;
As gentle as Dante the Poet, for only the lulls of the stress
Of the mightiest spirits can know it, this ineffable gentleness:

And then with the delicate tender fantastic dreamer of
      night,
Whose splendour is starlike splendour and his light a
      mystic moonlight,
Nocturn on nocturn dreaming while the mind floats far
      in the haze
And the dusk and the shadow and gleaming of a realm
      that has no days:
And then she sang ballads olden, ballads of love and of woe,
Love all burningly golden, grief with heart's-blood in its
      flow;
Those ballads of Scotland that thrill you, keen from the
      heart to the heart,
Till their pathos is seeming to kill you, with an exquisite
      bliss in the smart.

And then we went out of the valley and over the spur
      of the hill,
And down by a woodland alley where the sprinkled
      moonlight lay still;
For the breeze in the boughs was still and the breeze
      was still in the sprays,
And the leaves had scarcely a thrill in the stream of the
      silver rays,
But looked as if drawn on the sky or etched with a
      graver keen,
Sharp shadows thrown from on high deep out of the
      azure serene:

And a certain copse we knew, where never in Maytime
      fails,
While the night distils sweet dew, the song of the
      nightingales:
And there together we heard the lyrical drama of love

Of the wonderful passionate bird which swelleth the
  heart so above
All other thought of this life, all other care of this earth,
Be it of pleasure or strife, be it of sorrow or mirth,
Saving the one intense imperious passion supreme
Kindling the soul and the sense, making the world but
  a dream,
The dream of an aching delight and a yearning afar and afar,
While the music thrills all the void night to the loftiest
  pulsating star:—
'Love, love only, for ever; love with its torture and bliss;
All the world's glories can never equal two souls in one
  kiss.'

And when I had bidden farewell to my Love at the
  cottage door,
For a night and a day farewell, for a night and a day
  and no more,
I went down to the shining strand of our own belovèd bay,
To the shore of soft white sand caressed by the pure
  white spray,
In the arms of the hills serene, clothed from the base
  to the crest
With garments of manifold green, curving to east and
  to west;
And high in the pale blue south where the clouds were
  white as wool,
Over the little bay-mouth the moon shone near the full;
And I walked by the waves'soft moan, for my heart was
  beyond control,
And I needed to be alone with the night and my love
  and my soul,
And I could not think of sleep in the moonlight broad
  and clear,

For a music solemn and deep filled all my spirit's sphere,
A music interwoven of all that night I had heard,
From the music of mighty Beethoven to the song of the
    little brown bird.

And thus as I paced the shore beneath the azure abyss,
And my soul thrilled more and more with a yearning and
    sadness of bliss,
A voice came over the water from over the eastern cape,
Like the voice of some ocean daughter wailing a lover's
    escape,—
A voice so plaintive and distant, as faint as a wounded dove,
Whose wings are scarcely resistant to the air beneath and
    above,
Wavering, panting, urging from the farthest east to the west,
Over some wild sea surging in the hope forlorn of its nest;
A voice that quivered and trembled, with falls of a broken
    heart,
And then like that dove reassembled its forces to play
    out its part;
Till it came to a fall that was dying, the end of an in-
    finite grief,
A sobbing and throbbing and sighing that death was a
    welcome relief;
And so there was silence once more, and the moonlight
    looked sad as a pall,
And I stood entranced on the shore and marvelled
    what next would befall.

And thus all-expectant abiding I waited not long, for soon
A boat came gliding and gliding out in the light of the moon,
Gliding with muffled oars, slowly, a thin dark line,
Round from the shadowing shores into the silver shine
Of the clear moon westering now, and still drew on and on,

While the water before its prow breaking and glistering
    shone,
Slowly in silence strange; and the rower rowed till it lay
Afloat within easy range deep in the curve of the bay;
And besides the rower were two; a Woman, who sat in
    the stern,
And Her by her fame I knew, one of those fames that
    burn,
Startling and kindling the world, one whose likeness we
    everywhere see;
And a man reclining half-curled with an indolent grace
    at her knee,
The Signor, lord of her choice; and he lightly touched
    a guitar;——
A guitar for that glorious voice! Illumine the sun with
    a star!
She sat superb and erect, stately, all-happy, serene,
 Her right hand toying unchecked with the hair of that
    page of a Queen;
With her head and her throat and her bust like the bust
    and the throat and the head
Of Her who has long been dust, of Her who shall never
    be dead,
Preserved by the potent art made trebly potent by love,
While the transient ages depart from under the heavens
    above,—
Preserved in the colour and line on the canvas fulgently
    flung
By Him the Artist divine who triumphed and vanished
    so young:
Surely there rarely hath been a lot more to be envied in life
Than thy lot, O FORNARINA, whom RAPHAEL'S heart
    took to wife.

There was silence yet for a time save the tinkling Capricious
and quaint,
Then She lifted her voice sublime, no longer tender and faint,
Pathetic and tremulous, no! but firm as a column it rose,
Rising solemn and slow with a full rich swell to the close,
Firm as a marble column soaring with noble pride
In a triumph of rapture solemn to some Hero deified;
In a rapture of exultation made calm by its stress intense,
In a triumph of consecration and a jubilation immense.
And the Voice flowed on and on, and ever it swelled as
          it poured,
Till the stars that throbbed as they shone seemed
          throbbing with it in accord;
Till the moon herself in my dream, still Empress of all
          the night,
Was only that voice supreme translated into pure light:
And I lost all sense of the earth though I still had sense
          of the sea;
And I saw the stupendous girth of a tree like the Norse
          World-Tree;
And its branches filled all the sky, and the deep sea
          watered its root,
And the clouds were its leaves on high and the stars were
          its silver fruit;
Yet the stars were the notes of the singing and the moon
          was the voice of the song,
Through the vault of the firmament ringing and swelling
          resistlessly strong;
And the whole vast night was a shell for that music of
          manifold might,
And was strained by the stress of the swell of the music
          yet vaster than night.
And I saw as a crystal fountain whose shaft was a column
          of light

More high than the loftiest mountain ascend the abyss
    of the night;
And its spray filled all the sky, and the clouds were the
    clouds of its spray,
Which glittered in star-points on high and filled with pure
    silver the bay;
And ever in rising and falling it sang as it rose and it fell,
And the heavens with their pure azure walling all pulsed
    with the pulse of its swell,
For the stars were the notes of the singing and the moon
    was the voice of the song
Through the vault of the firmament ringing and swelling
    ineffably strong!
And the whole vast night was a shell for that music of
    manifold might,
And was strained by the stress of the swell of the music
    yet vaster than night:
And the fountain in swelling and soaring and filling beneath
    and above,
Grew flushed with red fire in outpouring, transmuting
    great power into love,
Great power with a greater love flushing, immense and
    intense and supreme,
As if all the World's heart-blood outgushing ensanguined
    the trance of my dream;
And the waves of its blood seemed to dash on the shore
    of the sky to the cope
With the stress of the fire of a passion and yearning of
    limitless scope.
Vast fire of a passion and yearning, keen torture of rapture
    intense,
A most unendurable burning consuming the soul with
    the sense:—
'Love, love only, for ever; love with its torture of bliss;

All the world's glories can never equal two souls in one kiss:
Love, and ever love wholly; love in all time and all space;
Life is consummate then solely in the death of a burning
    embrace.'

And at length when that Voice sank mute, and silence
    fell over all
Save the tinkling thin of that lute, the deep heavens
    rushed down like a pall,
The stars and the moon for a time with all their splendours
    of light,
Were quenched with that Voice sublime, and great darkness
    filled the night ....
When I felt again the scent of the night-flowers rich and
    sweet,
As ere my senses went, and knew where I stood on my feet,
And saw the yet-bright bay and the moon gone low in
    my dream,
The boat had passed away with Her the Singer supreme;
She was gone, the marvellous Singer whose wonderful
    world-wide fame
Could never possibly bring her a tithe of her just acclaim.
And I wandered all night in a trance of rapture and
    yearning and love,
And saw the dim grey expanse flush far with the dawning
    above;
And I passed that copse in the night, but the nightingales all
    were dumb
From their passionate aching delight, and perhaps whoever
    should come
On the morrow would find, I have read, under its bush
    or its tree
Some poor little brown bird dead, dead of its melody,
Slain by the agitation, by the stress and the strain of the strife,

And the pang of the vain emulation in the music yet
    dearer than life.
And I heard the skylarks singing high in the morning sun,
All the sunrise heavens ringing as the sunset heavens had done:
And ever I dreamed and pondered while over the fragrant
    soil,
My happy footsteps wandered before I resumed my toil:—
Truly, my darling, my Alice, truly the whole night long
Have I filled to the brim love's chalice with the wine of
    music and song.
I have passed and repassed your door from the singing
    until the dawn
A dozen times and more, and ever the curtains drawn;
And now that the morn is breaking out of the stillness deep,
Sweet as my visions of waking be all your visions of sleep!
Could you but wake, O my dearest, a moment, and give
    one glance,
Just a furtive peep the merest, to learn the day's advance!
For I must away up the dale and over the hill to my toil,
And the night's rich dreams grow pale in the working
    day's turmoil;
But to-night, O my darling, my Alice, till night it will not
    be long,
We will fill to the brim love's chalice with the wine of
    music and song;
And never the memory fails of what I have learnt in my dream
From the song of the nightingales and the song of the
    Singer supreme:—
'Love, love only, for ever; love with its torture and bliss;
All the world's glories can never equal two souls in one kiss:
Love, love ever and wholly; love in all time and all space;
Love is consummate then solely in the death of a burning
embrace.'

To Our Ladies Of Death*

'Tired with all these, for restful death I cry.'
SHAKESPEARE: *Sonnet 66.*

Weary of erring in this desert Life,
  Weary of hoping hopes for ever vain,
Weary of struggling in all-sterile strife,
  Weary of thought which maketh nothing plain,
I close my eyes and calm my panting breath,
And pray to Thee, O ever-quiet Death!
  To come and soothe away my bitter pain.

The strong shall strive, —may they be victors crowned;
  The wise still seek, —may they at length find Truth;
The young still hope, —may purest love be found
  To make their age more glorious than their youth.
For me; my brain is weak, my heart is cold,
My hope and faith long dead; my life but bold
  In jest and laugh to parry hateful ruth.

Over me pass the days and months and years
  Like squadrons and battalions of the foe
Trampling with thoughtless thrusts and alien jeers
  Over a wounded soldier lying low:
He grips his teeth, or flings them words of scorn
To mar their triumph: but the while, outworn,
  Inwardly craves for death to end his woe.

Thus I, in secret, call, O Death! to Thee,
  Thou youngest of the solemn Sisterhood,
Thou Gentlest of the mighty Sisters Three
  Whom I have known so well since first endued
By Love and Grief with vision to discern

What spiritual life doth throb and burn
  Through all our world, with evil powers and good.

The Three whom I have known so long, so well,
  By intimate communion, face to face,
In every mood, of Earth, of Heaven, of Hell,
  In every season and in every place,
That joy of Life has ceased to visit me,
As one estranged by powerful witchery,
  Infatuate in a Siren's weird embrace.

First Thou, O priestess, prophetess, and queen,
  Our Lady of Beatitudes, first Thou:
Of mighty stature, of seraphic mien,
  Upon the tablet of whose broad white brow
Unvanquishable Truth is written clear,
The secret of the mystery of our sphere,
  The regnant word of the Eternal Now.

Thou standest garmented in purest white;
  But from thy shoulders wings of power half-spread
Invest thy form with such miraculous light
  As dawn may clothe the earth with: and, instead
Of any jewel-kindled golden crown,
The glory of thy long hair flowing down
  Is dazzling noonday sunshine round thy head.

Upon a sword thy left hand resteth calm,
  A naked sword, two-edged and long and straight;
A branch of olive with a branch of palm
  Thy right hand proffereth to hostile Fate.
The shining plumes that clothe thy feet are bound
By knotted strings, as if to tread the ground
  With weary steps when thou wouldst soar elate.

Twin heavens uplifted to the heavens, thine eyes
  Are solemn with unutterable thought
And love and aspiration; yet there lies
  Within their light eternal sadness, wrought
By hope deferred and baffled tenderness:
Of all the souls whom thou dost love and bless,
  How few revere and love thee as they ought!

Thou leadest heroes from their warfare here
  To nobler fields where grander crowns are won;
Thou leadest sages from this twilight sphere
  To cloudless heavens and an unsetting sun;
Thou leadest saints unto that purer air
Whose breath is spiritual life and prayer!
  Yet, lo! they seek thee not, but fear and shun!

Thou takest to thy most maternal breast
  Young children from the desert of this earth,
Ere sin hath stained their souls, or grief opprest,
  And bearest them unto an heavenly birth,
To be the Vestals of God's Fane above:
And yet their kindred moan against thy love,
  With wild and selfish moans in bitter dearth.

Most holy Spirit, first Self-conqueror;
  Thou Victress over Time and Destiny
And Evil, in the all-deciding war
So fierce, so long, so dreadful! —Would that me
Thou hadst upgathered in my life's pure morn!
Unworthy then, less worthy now, forlorn,
  I dare not, Gracious Mother, call on Thee.

Next Thou, O sibyl, sorceress and queen,
  Our Lady of Annihilation, Thou!

Of mighty stature, of demoniac mien;
  Upon whose swarthy face and livid brow
Are graven deeply anguish, malice, scorn,
Strength ravaged by unrest, resolve forlorn
  Of any hope, dazed pride that will not bow.

Thy form is clothed with wings of iron gloom;
  But round about thee, like a chain, is rolled,
Cramping the sway of every mighty plume,
  A stark constringent serpent fold on fold:
Of its two heads, one sting is in thy brain,
The other in thy heart; their venom-pain
  Like fire distilling through thee uncontrolled.

A rod of serpents wieldeth thy right hand;
  Thy left a cup of raging fire, whose light
Burns lurid on thyself as thou dost stand;
  Thy lidless eyes tenebriously bright;
Thy wings, thy vestures, thy dishevelled hair
Dark as the Grave; thou statue of Despair,
  Thou Night essential radiating night.

Thus have I seen thee in thine actual form;
  Not thus can see thee those whom thou dost sway,
Inscrutable Enchantress: young and warm,
  Pard-beautiful and brilliant, ever gay;
Thy cup the very Wine of Life, thy rod
The wand of more voluptuous spells than God
  Can wield in Heaven; thus charmest thou thy prey.

The selfish, fatuous, proud, and pitiless,
  All who have falsified life's royal trust;
The strong whose strength hath basked in idleness,
  The great heart given up to worldly lust,

The great mind destitute of moral faith;
Thou scourgest down to Night and utter Death,
  Or penal spheres of retribution just.

O mighty Spirit, fraudful and malign,
  Demon of madness and perversity!
The evil passions which may make me thine
Are not yet irrepressible in me;
  And I have pierced thy mark of riant youth,
And seen thy form in all its hideous truth:
  I will not, Dreadful Mother, call on Thee.

Last Thou, retirèd nun and throneless queen,
  Our Lady of Oblivion, last Thou:
Of human stature, of abstracted mien;
  Upon whose pallid face and drooping brow
Are shadowed melancholy dreams of Doom,
And deep absorption into silent gloom,
  And weary bearing of the heavy Now.

Thou art all shrouded in a gauzy veil,
  Sombrous and cloudlike; all, except that face
Of subtle loveliness though weirdly pale.
  Thy soft, slow-gliding footsteps leave no trace,
And stir no sound. Thy drooping hands infold
Their frail white fingers; and, unconscious, hold
  A poppy-wreath, thine anodyne of grace.

Thy hair is like a twilight round thy head:
  Thine eyes are shadowed wells, from Lethe-stream
With drowsy subterranean waters fed;
  Obscurely deep, without a stir or gleam;
The gazer drinks in from them with his gaze
An opiate charm to curtain all his days,
  A passive languor of oblivious dream.

Thou hauntest twilight regions, and the trance
  Of moonless nights when stars are few and wan:
Within black woods; or over the expanse
  Of desert seas abysmal; or upon
Old solitary shores whose populous graves
  Are rocked in rest by ever-moaning waves;
  Or through vast ruined cities still and lone.

The weak, the weary, and the desolate,
  The poor, the mean, the outcast, the opprest,
All trodden down beneath the march of Fate,
  Thou gatherest, loving Sister, to thy breast,
Soothing their pain and weariness asleep;
Then in thy hidden Dreamland hushed and deep
  Dost lay them, shrouded in eternal rest.

O sweetest Sister, and sole Patron Saint
  Of all the humble eremites who flee
From out life's crowded tumult, stunned and faint,
  To seek a stern and lone tranquillity
In Libyan wastes of time: my hopeless life
With famished yearning craveth rest from strife;
  Therefore, thou Restful One, I call on Thee!

Take me, and lull me into perfect sleep;
  Down, down, far-hidden in thy duskiest cave;
While all the clamorous years above me sweep
  Unheard, or, like the voice of seas that rave
On far-off coasts, but murmuring o'er my trance,
A dim vast monotone, that shall enhance
  The restful rapture of the inviolate grave.

Upgathered thus in thy divine embrace,
  Upon mine eyes thy soft mesmeric hand,

While wreaths of opiate odour interlace
  About my pulseless brow; babe-pure and bland,
Passionless, senseless, thoughtless, let me dream
Some ever-slumbrous, never-varying theme,
  Within the shadow of thy Timeless Land.

That when I thus have drunk my inmost fill
  Of perfect peace, I may arise renewed;
In soul and body, intellect and will,
  Equal to cope with Life whate'er its mood;
To sway its storm and energise its calm;
Through rhythmic years evolving like a psalm
  Of infinite love and faith and sanctitude.

But if this cannot be, no less I cry,
  Come, lead me with thy terrorless control
Down to our Mother's bosom, there to die
  By abdication of my separate soul:
So shall this single, self-impelling piece
Of mechanism from lone labour cease,
  Resolving into union with the Whole.

Our Mother feedeth thus our little life,
  That we in turn may feed her with our death:
The great Sea sways, one interwoven strife,
  Wherefrom the Sun exhales a subtle breath,
To float the heavens sublime in form and hue,
Then turning cold and dark in order due
  Rain weeping back to swell the Sea beneath.

One part of me shall feed a little worm,
  And it a bird on which a man may feed;
One lime the mould, one nourish insect-sperm;
  One thrill sweet grass, one pulse in bitter weed;

This swell a fruit, and that evolve in air;
Another trickle to a springlet's lair,
  Another paint a daisy on the mead:

With cosmic interchange of parts for all,
  Through all the modes of being numberless
Of every element, as may befall.
  And if earth's general soul hath consciousness,
Their new life must with strange new joy be thrilled,
Of perfect law all perfectly fulfilled;
  No sin, no fear, no failure, no excess.

Weary of living isolated life,
  Weary of hoping hopes for ever vain,
Weary of struggling in all-sterile strife,
  Weary of thought which maketh nothing plain,
I close my eyes and hush my panting breath,
And yearn for Thee, divinely tranquil Death,
  To come and soothe away my bitter pain.

* The Three Ladies suggested by the sublime sisterhood of Our Ladies of Sorrow, in the
'Suspiria de Profundis' of De Quincey.

Insomnia

I HEARD the sounding of the midnight hour;
  The others one by one had left the room,
In calm assurance that the gracious power
  Of sleep's fine alchemy would bless the gloom,
Transmuting all its leaden weight to gold,
To treasures of rich virtues manifold,
    New strength, new health, new life:
Just weary enough to nestle softly, sweetly,
Into divine unconsciousness, completely
Delivered from the world of toil and care and strife.

Just weary enough to feel assured of rest,
  Of Sleep's divine oblivion and repose,
Renewing heart and brain for richer zest
  Of waking life when golden morning glows,
As young and pure and glad as if the first
That ever on the void of darkness burst
    With ravishing warmth and light;
On dewy grass and flowers and blithe birds singing,
And shining waters, all enraptured springing,
Fragrance and shine and song, out of the womb of night.

But I with infinite weariness outworn,
  Haggard with endless nights unblessed by sleep,
Ravaged by thoughts unutterably forlorn,
  Plunged in despairs unfathomably deep,
Went cold and pale and trembling with affright
Into the desert vastitude of Night,
    Arid and wild and black;

Foreboding no oasis of sweet slumber,
Counting beforehand all the countless number
Of sands that are its minutes on my desolate track

And so I went, the last, to my drear bed,
  Aghast as one who should go down to lie
Among the blissfully unconscious dead,
  Assured that as the endless years flowed by
Over the dreadful silence and deep gloom
And dense oppression of the stifling tomb,
    He only of them all,
Nerveless and impotent to madness, never
Could hope oblivion's perfect trance for ever:
An agony of life eternal in death's pall.

But that would be for ever, without cure!—
  And yet the agony be not more great;
Supreme fatigue and pain, while they endure,
  Into Eternity their time translate;
Be it of hours and days or countless years,
And boundless aeons, it alike appears
    To the crushed victim's soul;
Utter despair foresees no termination,
But feels itself of infinite duration;
The smallest fragment instant comprehends the whole.

The absolute of torture as of bliss
  Is timeless, each transcending time and space;
The one an infinite obscure abyss,
  The other an eternal Heaven of grace.—
Keeping a little lamp of glimmering light
Companion through the horror of the night,
    I laid me down aghast
As *he* of all who pass death's quiet portal

Malignantly reserved alone immortal,
In consciousness of bale that must for ever last.

I laid me down and closed my heavy eyes,
  As if sleep's mockery might win true sleep;
And grew aware, with awe but not surprise,
  Blindly aware through all the silence deep,
Of some dark Presence watching by my bed,
The awful image of a nameless dread;
    But I lay still fordone;
And felt its Shadow on me dark and solemn
And steadfast as a monumental column,
And thought drear thoughts of Doom, and heard the
    bells chime One.

And then I raised my weary eyes and saw,
  By some slant moonlight on the ceiling thrown
And faint lamp-gleam, that Image of my awe,
  Still as a pillar of basaltic stone,
But all enveloped in a sombre shroud
Except the wan face drooping heavy-browed,
    With sad eyes fixed on mine;
Sad weary yearning eyes, but fixed remorseless
Upon my eyes yet wearier, that were forceless
To bear the cruel pressure; cruel, unmalign.

Wherefore I asked for what I knew too well:
  O ominous midnight Presence, What art Thou?
Whereto in tones that sounded like a knell:
  'I am the Second Hour, appointed now
To watch beside thy slumberless unrest.'
Then I: Thus both, unlike, alike unblest;
    For I should sleep, you fly:
Are not those wings beneath thy mantle moulded?

O Hour! unfold those wings so straitly folded,
And urge thy natural flight beneath the moonlit sky.

'My wings shall open when your eyes shall close
   In real slumber from this waking drear;
Your wild unrest is my enforced repose;
   Ere I move hence you must not know me here.'
Could not your wings fan slumber through my brain,
Soothing away its weariness and pain?
    'Your sleep must stir my wings:
Sleep, and I bear you gently on my pinions
Athwart my span of hollow night's dominions,
Whence hour on hour shall bear to morning's golden springs.'

That which I ask of you, you ask of me,
   O weary Hour, thus standing sentinel
Against your nature, as I feel and see
   Against my own your form immovable:
Could I bring Sleep to set you on the wing,
What other thing so gladly would I bring?
    Truly the poet saith:
If that is best whose absence we deplore most,
Whose presence in our longings is the foremost,
What blessings equal Sleep save only love and death?

I let my lids fall, sick of thought and sense,
   But felt that Shadow heavy on my heart;
And saw the night before me an immense
   Black waste of ridge- walls, hour by hour apart,
Dividing deep ravines: from ridge to ridge
Sleep's flying hour was an aërial bridge;
    But I, whose hours stood fast,
Must climb down painfully each steep side hither,
And climb more painfully each steep side thither,
And so make one hour's span for years of travail last.

Thus I went down into that first ravine,
  Wearily, slowly, blindly, and alone,
Staggering, stumbling, sinking depths unseen.
  Shaken and bruised and gashed by stub and stone;
And at the bottom paven with slipperiness,
A torrent-brook rushed headlong with such stress
    Against my feeble limbs,
Such fury of wave and foam and icy bleakness
Buffeting insupportably my weakness
That when I would recall dazed memory swirls and swims.

How I got through I know not, faint as death;
  And then I had to climb the awful scarp,
Creeping with many a pause for panting breath.
  Clinging to tangled root and rock -jut sharp;
Perspiring with faint chills instead of heat,
Trembling, and bleeding hands and knees and feet;
    Falling, to rise anew;
Until, with lamentable toil and travel
Upon the ridge of arid sand and gravel
I lay supine half-dead and heard the bells chime Two;

And knew a change of Watchers in the room
  Without a stir or sound beside my bed;
Only the tingling silence of the gloom.
  The muffled pulsing of the night's deep dread;
And felt an image mightier to appal,
And looked; the moonlight on the bed-foot wall
    And corniced ceiling white
Was slanting now; and in the midst stood solemn
And hopeless as a black sepulchral column
A steadfast shrouded Form, the Third Hour of the night.

The fixed regard implacably austere,
  Yet none the less ineffably forlorn.
Something transcending all my former fear
  Came jarring through my shattered frame outworn:
I knew that crushing rock could not be stirred;
I had no heart to say a single word,
  But closed my eyes again:
And set me shuddering to the task stupendous
Of climbing down and up that gulf tremendous
Unto the next hour-ridge beyond Hope's farthest ken.

Men sigh and plain and wail how life is brief:
  Ah yes, our bright eternities of bliss
Are transient, rare, minute beyond belief,
  Mere star-dust meteors in Time's night-abyss;
Ah no, our black eternities intense
Of bale are lasting, dominant, immense,
  As time which is their breath;
The memory of the bliss is yearning sorrow,
The memory of the bale clouds every morrow
Darkening through nights and days unto the night of Death.

No human words could paint my travail sore
  In the thick darkness of the next ravine,
Deeper immeasurably than that before:
  When hideous agonies, unheard, unseen,
In overwhelming floods of torture roll,
And horrors of great darkness drown the soul,
  To be is not to be
In memory save as ghastliest impression,
And chaos of demoniacal possession ....
I shuddered on the ridge, and heard the bells chime Three.

And like a pillar of essential gloom,
  Most terrible in stature and regard,
Black in the moonlight filling all the room
  The image of the Fourth Hour, evil-starred,
Stood over me; but there was Something more,
Something behind It undiscerned before,
    More dreadful than Its dread,
Which overshadowed it as with a fateful
Inexorable fascination hateful,—
A wan and formless Shade from regions of the dead.

  I shut my eyes against that spectral Shade,
    Which yet allured me with a deadly charm;
  And that black Image of the Hour, dismayed
    By such tremendous menacing of harm;
  And so into the gulph as into Hell;
  Where what immeasurable depths I fell,
      With seizures of the heart
  Whose each clutch seemed the end of all pulsation,
  And tremors of exanimate prostration,
Are horrors in my soul that never can depart.

  If I for hope or wish had any force,
    It was that I might rush down sharply hurled
  From rock to rock until a mangled corse
    Down with the fury of the torrent whirled,
  The fury of black waters and white foam,
  To where the homeless find their only home,
      In the immense void Sea,
  Whose isles are worlds, surrounding, unsurrounded,
  Whose depths no mortal plummet ever sounded,
Beneath all surface storm calm in Eternity.

Such hope or wish was as a feeble spark,
  A little lamp's pale glimmer in a tomb,
To just reveal the hopeless deadly dark
  And wordless horrors of my soul's fixed doom:
Yet some mysterious instinct obstinate,
Blindly unconscious as a law of Fate,
    Still urged me on and bore
My shattered being through the unfeared peril
Of death less hateful than the life as sterile:
I shuddered on the ridge, and heard the bells chime Four.

The Image of that Fifth Hour of the night
  Was blacker in the moonlight now aslant
Upon its left than on its shrouded right:
  And over and behind it, dominant,
The shadow not Its shadow cast its spell,
Most vague and dim and wan and terrible,
    Death's ghastly aureole,
Pregnant with overpowering fascination,
Commanding by repulsive instigation,
Despair's envenomed anodyne to tempt the Soul.

I closed my eyes, but could no longer keep
  Under that Image and most awful Shade,
Supine in mockery of blissful sleep,
  Delirious with such fierce thirst unallayed:
Of all worst agonies the most unblest
Is passive agony of wild unrest:
    Trembling and faint I rose,
And dressed with painful efforts, and descended
With furtive footsteps and with breath suspended,
And left the slumbering house with my unslumbering woes.

Constrained to move through the unmoving hours,
  Accurst from rest because the hours stood still;
Feeling the hands of the Infernal Powers
  Heavy upon me for enormous ill,
Inscrutable intolerable pain,
Against which mortal pleas and prayers are vain,
  Gaspings of dying breath,
And human struggles, dying spasms yet vainer:
Renounce defence when Doom is the Arraigner;
Let impotence of Life subside appeased in Death.

I paced the silent and deserted streets
  In cold dark shade and chillier moonlight grey;
Pondering a dolorous series of defeats
  And black disasters from life's opening day,
Invested with the shadow of a doom
That filled the Spring and Summer with a gloom
  Most wintry bleak and drear;
Gloom from within as from a sulphurous censer
Making the glooms without for ever denser,
To blight the buds and flowers and fruitage of my year.

Against a bridge's stony parapet
  I leaned, and gazed into the waters black;
And marked an angry morning red and wet
  Beneath a livid and enormous rack
Glare out confronting the belated moon,
Huddled and wan and feeble as the swoon
  Of featureless Despair:
When some stray workman, half-asleep but lusty,
Passed urgent through the rainpour wild and gusty,
I felt a ghost already, planted watching there.

As phantom to its grave, or to its den
　　Some wild beast of the night when night is sped,
I turned unto my homeless home again
　　To front a day only less charged with dread
Than that dread night; and after day, to front
Another night of—what would be the brunt?
　　　I put the thought aside,
To be resumed when common life unfolded
In common daylight had my brain remoulded;
Meanwhile the flaws of rain refreshed and fortified.

The day passed, and the night; and other days,
　　And other nights; and all of evil doom;
The sun-hours in a sick bewildering haze,
　　The star-hours in a thick enormous gloom,
With rending lightnings and with thunder-knells;
The ghastly hours of all the timeless Hells:—
　　　Bury them with their bane!
I look back on the words already written,
And writhe by cold rage stung, by self-scorn smitten,
They are so weak and vain and infinitely inane. . . .

'How from those hideous Malebolges deep
　　I ever could win back to upper earth,
Restored to human nights of blessed sleep
　　And healthy waking with the new day's birth?'—
How do men climb back from a swoon whose stress,
Crushing far deeper than all consciousness,
　　　Is deep as deep death seems?
Who can the steps and stages mete and number
By which we re-emerge from nightly slumber?
Our poor vast petty life is one dark maze of dreams.

In The Room

'Ceste insigne fable et tragicque comedie.'
                                        - RABELAIS.

THE sun was down, and twilight grey
  Filled half the air; but in the room,
Whose curtain had been drawn all day,
  The twilight was a dusky gloom:
Which seemed at first as still as death,
  And void; but was indeed all rife
With subtle thrills, the pulse and breath
  Of multitudinous lower life.

In their abrupt and headlong way
  Bewildered flies for light had dashed
Against the curtain all the day,
  And now slept wintrily abashed;
And nimble mice slept, wearied out
  With such a double night's uproar;
But solid beetles crawled about
  The chilly hearth and naked floor.

And so throughout the twilight hour
  That vaguely murmurous hush and rest
There brooded; and beneath its power
  Life throbbing held its throbs supprest:
Until the thin-voiced mirror sighed,
  I am all blurred with dust and damp,
So long ago the clear day died,
  So long has gleamed nor fire nor lamp.

Whereon the curtain murmured back,
  Some change is on us, good or ill;

Behind me and before is black
  As when those human things lie still:
But I have seen the darkness grow
  As grows the daylight every morn;
Have felt out there long shine and glow,
  In here long chilly dusk forlorn.

The cupboard grumbled with a groan,
  Each new day worse starvation brings:
Since *he* came here I have not known
  Or sweets or cates or wholesome things:
But now! a pinch of meal, a crust,
  Throughout the week is all I get.
I am so empty; it is just
  As when they said we were to let.

What is become, then, of our Man?
  The petulant old glass exclaimed;
If all this time he slumber can,
  He really ought to be ashamed.
I wish we had our Girl again,
  So gay and busy, bright and fair:
The girls are better than these men,
  Who only for their dull selves care.

It is so many hours ago—
  The lamp and fire were both alight—
I saw him pacing to and fro,
  Perturbing restlessly the night.
His face was pale to give one fear,
  His eyes when lifted looked too bright;
He muttered; what, I could not hear:
  Bad words though; something was not right.

The table said, He wrote so long
  That I grew weary of his weight;
The pen kept up a cricket song,
  It ran and ran at such a rate:
And in the longer pauses he
  With both his folded arms downpressed,
And stared as one who does not see,
  Or sank his head upon his breast.

The fire-grate said, I am as cold
  As if I never had a blaze;
The few dead cinders here I hold,
  I held unburned for days and days.
Last night he made them flare; but still
  What good did all his writing do?
Among my ashes curl and thrill
  Thin ghosts of all those papers too.

The table answered, Not quite all;
  He saved and folded up one sheet,
And sealed it fast, and let it fall;
  And here it lies now white and neat.
Whereon the letter's whisper came,
  My writing is closed up too well;
Outside there's not a single name,
  And who should read me I can't tell.

The mirror sneered with scornful spite,
  (That ancient crack which spoiled her looks
Had marred her temper), Write and write!
  And read those stupid, worn-out books!
That's all he does, read, write, and read,
  And smoke that nasty pipe which stinks:
He never takes the slightest heed
  How any of us feels or thinks.

But Lucy fifty times a day
  Would come and smile here in my face,
Adjust a tress that curled astray,
  Or tie a ribbon with more grace:
She looked so young and fresh and fair,
  She blushed with such a charming bloom,
It did one good to see her there,
  And brightened all things in the room.

She did not sit hours stark and dumb
  As pale as moonshine by the lamp;
To lie in bed when day was come,
  And leave us curtained chill and damp.
She slept away the dreary dark,
  And rose to greet the pleasant morn;
And sang as gaily as a lark
  While busy as the flies sun-born.

And how she loved us every one;
  And dusted this and mended that,
With trills and laughs and freaks of fun,
  And tender scoldings in her chat!
And then her bird, that sang as shrill
  As she sang sweet; her darling flowers
That grew there in the window-sill,
  Where she would sit at work for hours.

It was not much she ever wrote;
  Her fingers had good work to do;
Say, once a week a pretty note;
  And very long it took her too.
And little more she read, I wis;
  Just now and then a pictured sheet,
Besides those letters she would kiss
  And croon for hours, they were so sweet.

She had her friends too, blithe young girls,
  Who whispered, babbled, laughed, caressed,
And romped and danced with dancing curls,
  And gave our life a joyous zest.
But with this dullard, glum and sour,
  Not one of all his fellow-men
Has ever passed a social hour;
  We might be in some wild beast's den.

This long tirade aroused the bed,
  Who spoke in deep and ponderous bass,
Befitting that calm life be led,
  As if firm-rooted in his place:
In broad majestic bulk alone,
  As in thrice venerable age,
He stood at once the royal throne,
  The monarch, the experienced sage:

I know what is and what has been;
  Not anything to me comes strange,
Who in so many years have seen
  And lived through every kind of change.
I know when men are good or bad,
  When well or ill, he slowly said;
When sad or glad, when sane or mad,
  And when they sleep alive or dead.

At this last word of solemn lore
  A tremor circled through the gloom,
As if a crash upon the floor
  Had jarred and shaken all the room:
For nearly all the listening things
  Were old and worn, and knew what curse
Of violent change death often brings,
  From good to bad, from bad to worse;

They get to know each other well,
  To feel at home and settled down;
Death bursts among them like a shell,
  And strews them over all the town.
The bed went on, This man who lies
  Upon me now is stark and cold;
He will not any more arise,
  And do the things he did of old.

But we shall have short peace or rest;
  For soon up here will come a rout,
And nail him in a queer long chest,
  And carry him like luggage out.
They will be muffled all in black,
  And whisper much, and sigh and weep:
But he will never more come back,
  And some one else in me must sleep.

Thereon a little phial shrilled,
  Here empty on the chair I lie:
I heard one say, as I was filled,
  With half of this a man would die.
The man there drank me with slow breath,
  And murmured, Thus ends barren strife:
O sweeter, thou cold wine of death,
  Than ever sweet warm wine of life.

One of my cousins long ago,
  A little thing, the mirror said,
Was carried to a couch to show,
  Whether a man was really dead.
Two great improvements marked the case:
  He did not blur her with his breath,
His many-wrinkled, twitching face
  Was smooth old ivory: verdict, Death.

It lay, the lowest thing there, lulled
  Sweet-sleep-like in corruption's truce;
The form whose purpose was annulled,
  While all the other shapes meant use.
It lay, the *he* become now *it*,
  Unconscious of the deep disgrace,
Unanxious how its parts might flit
  Through what new forms in time and space.

It lay and preached, as dumb things do,
  More powerfully than tongues can prate;
Though life be torture through and through,
  Man is but weak to plain of fate:
The drear path crawls on drearier still
  To wounded feet and hopeless breast?
Well, he can lie down when he will,
  And straight all ends in endless rest

And while the black night nothing saw,
  And till the cold morn came at last,
That old bed held the room in awe
  With tales of its experience vast.
It thrilled the gloom; it told such tales
  Of human sorrows and delights,
Of fever moans and infant wails,
  Of births and deaths and bridal nights.

The Naked Goddess

THROUGH the country to the town
Ran a rumour and renown,
That a woman grand and tall,
Swift of foot, and therewithal
Naked as a lily gleaming,
Had been seen by eyes not dreaming,
Darting down far forest glades,
Flashing sunshine through the shades.

With this rumour's swelling word
All the city buzzed and stirred;
Solemn senators conferred;
Priest, astrologer, and mage,
Subtle sophist, bard, and sage,
Brought their wisdom, lore, and wit,
To expound or riddle it:
Last a porter ventured—'We
Might go out ourselves to see.'

Thus, upon a summer morn
Lo the city all forlorn;
Every house and street and square
In the sunshine still and bare,
Every galley left to sway
Silent in the glittering bay;
All the people swarming out,
Young and old a joyous rout,

Rich and poor, far-streaming through
Fields and meadows dank with dew,
Crowd on crowd, and throng on throng;
Chatter, laughter, jest, and song
Deafened all the singing birds,
Wildered sober grazing herds.

  Up the hillside 'gainst the sun,
Where the forest outskirts run;
On along the level high,
Where the azure of the sky,
And the ruddy morning sheen,
Drop in fragments through the treen,
Where the sward surrounds the brake
With a lucid, glassy lake,
Where the ample glades extend
Until clouds and foliage blend;
Where whoever turneth may
See the city and the bay,
And, beyond, the broad sea bright,
League on league of slanting light;
Where the moist blue shadows sleep
In the sacred forest deep.

  Suddenly the foremost pause,
Ere the rear discern a cause;
Loiterers press up row on row,
All the mass heaves to and fro;
All seem murmuring in one strain,
All seem hearkening fixed and fain:
Silence, and the lifted light
Of countless faces gazing white.

Four broad beech-trees, great of bole,
Crowned the green, smooth-swelling knoll;
There She leant, the glorious form
Dazzling with its beauty warm,
Naked as the sun of noon,
Naked as the midnight moon:
And around her, tame and mild,
All the forest creatures wild—
Lion, panther, kid, and fawn,
Eagle, hawk, and dove, all drawn
By the magic of her splendour,
By her great voice, rich and tender,
Whereof every beast and bird
Understood each tone and word,
While she fondled and carest,
Playing freaks of joyous zest.

Suddenly the lion stood,
Turned and saw the multitude,
Swelled his mighty front in ire,
Roared the roar of raging fire:
Then She turned, the living light,
Sprang erect, grew up in height,
Smote them with the flash and blaze
Of her terrible, swift gaze;
A divine, flushed, throbbing form,
Dreafuller than blackest storm.

All the forest creatures cowered,
Trembling, moaning, overpowered;
All the simple folk who saw
Sank upon their knees in awe
Of this Goddess, fierce and splendid,
Whom they witless had offended:

And they murmured out faint prayers,
Inarticulate despairs,
Till her hot and angry mien
Grew more gentle and serene.

  Stood the high priest forth, and went
Halfway up the green ascent:
There began a preachment long
Of the great and grievous wrong
She unto her own soul wrought
In thus living without thought
Of the gods who sain and save,
Of the life beyond the grave:
Living with the beasts that perish,
Far from all the rites that cherish
Hope and faith and holy love,
And appease the thrones above:
Full of unction pled the preacher;
Let her come and they would teach her
Spirit strangled in the mesh
Of the vile and sinful flesh,
How to gain the heavenly prize,
How grow meet for Paradise;
Penance, prayer, self-sacrifice,
Fasting, cloistered solitude,
Mind uplifted, heart subdued;
Thus a Virgin, clean and chaste,
In the Bridegroom's arms embraced.
Vestal sister's hooded gown,
Straight and strait, of dismal brown,
Here he proffered, and laid down
On the green grass like a frown.

Then stood forth the old arch-sage,
Wrinkled more with thought than age:
What could worse afflict, deject
Any well-trained intellect
Than in savage forest seeing
Such a full-grown human being
With the beasts and birds at play,
Ignorant and wild as they?
Sciences and arts, by which
Man makes Nature's poor life rich,
Dominates the world around,
Proves himself its King self-crowned,
She knew nothing of them, she
Knew not even what they be!
Body naked to the air,
And the reason just as bare;
Yet (since circumstance, that can
Hinder the full growth of man,
Cannot kill the seeds of worth
Innate in the Lord of Earth),
Yet she might be taught and brought
To. full sovranty of thought,
Crowned with reason's glorious crown.
So he tendered and laid down,
Sober grey beside the brown,
Amplest philosophic gown.

Calm and proud she stood the while
With a certain wondering smile;
When the luminous sage was done
She began to speak as one
Using language not her own,
Simplest words in sweetest tone:
'Poor old greybeards, worn and bent!

I do know not what they meant;
Only here and there a word
Reached my mind of all I heard;
Let some child come here, I may
Understand what it can say.'

  So two little children went,
Lingering up the green ascent,
Hand in hand, but grew the while
Bolder in her gentle smile;
When she kissed them they were free,
Joyous as at mother's knee.
'Tell me, darlings, now,' said she,
'What they want to say to me.'
Boy and girl then, nothing loth,
Sometimes one and sometimes both,
Prattled to her sitting there
Fondling with their soft young hair:
'Dear kind lady, do you stay
Here with always holiday?
Do you sleep among the trees?
People want you, if you please,
To put on your dress and come
With us to the City home;
Live with us and be our friend:
Oh, such pleasant times we'll spend! . . .
But if you can't come away,
Will you let us stop and play
With you and all these happy things
With hair and horns and shining wings?'

  She arose and went half down,
Took the vestal sister's gown,
Tried it on, burst through its shroud,

As the sun burns through a cloud:
Flung it from her split and rent;
Said: 'This cerement sad was meant
For some creatures stunted, thin,
Breastless, blighted, bones and skin.'

Then the sage's robe she tried,
Muffling in its long folds wide
All her lithe and glorious grace:
'I should stumble every pace!
This big bag was meant to hold
Some poor sluggard fat and old,
Limping, shuffling wearily,
With a form not fit to see!'
So she flung it off again
With a gesture of disdain.

Naked as the midnight moon,
Naked as the sun of noon,
Burning too intensely bright,
Clothed in its own dazzling light;
Seen less thus than in the shroud
Of morning mist or evening cloud;
She stood terrible and proud
O'er the pallid quivering crowd.

At a gesture ere they wist,
Perched a falcon on her wrist,
And she whispered to the bird
Something it alone there heard;
Then she threw it off: when thrown
Straight it rose as falls a stone,
Arrow-swift on high, on high,
Till a mere speck in the sky;

Then it circled round and round,
Till, as if the prey were found,
Forth it darted on its quest
Straight away into the West....
Every eye that watched its flight
Felt a sideward flash of light,
All were for a moment dazed:
Then around intently gazed;
What had passed them? Where was She,
The offended deity?
O'er the city, o'er the bay,
They beheld her melt away,
Melt away beyond their quest
Through the regions of the west;
While the eagle screamed rauque ire,
And the lion roared like fire.

    That same night both priest and sage
Died accursed in sombre rage.
Never more in wild wood green
Was that glorious Goddess seen,
Never more: and from that day
Evil hap and dull decay
Fell on countryside and town;
Life and vigour dwindled down;
Storms in Spring nipped bud and sprout,
Summer suns shed plague and drought,
Autumn's store was crude and scant,
Winter snows beleaguered want;
Vines were black at vintage-tide,
Flocks and herds of murrain died;
Fishing boats came empty home,
Good ships foundered in the foam;
Haggard traders lost all heart

Wandering through the empty mart:
For the air hung thick with gloom,
Silence, and the sense of doom.

  But those little children she
Had caressed so tenderly
Were betrothed that self-same night
Grew up beautiful and bright,
Lovers through the years of play
Forward to their marriage-day.
Three long moons of bridal bliss
Overflowed them; after this,
With his bride and with a band
Of the noblest in the land,
Youths and maidens, wedded pairs
Scarcely older in life's cares,
He took ship and sailed away
Westward Ho from out the bay:
Portioned from their native shrine
With the Sacred Fire divine,
They will cherish while they roam,
Quenchless 'mid the salt sea foam,
Till it burns beneath a dome
In some new and far-off home.

  As they ventured more and more
In that ocean without shore,
And some hearts were growing cold
At the emprise all too bold,
It is said a falcon came
Down the void blue swift as flame;
Every sunset came to rest
On the prow's high curving crest,
Every sunrise rose from rest

Flying forth into the west;
And they followed, faint no more,
Through that ocean without shore.

   Three moons crescent fill and wane
O'er the solitary main,
When behold a green shore smile:
It was that Atlantic isle,
Drowned beneath the waves and years,
Whereof some faint shadow peers
Dubious through the modern stream
Of Platonic legend-dream.
High upon that green shore stood
She who left their native wood;
Glorious, and with solemn hand
Beckoned to them there to land.
Though She forthwith disappeared
As the wave-worn galley neared,
They knew well her presence still
Haunted stream and wood and hill.
There they landed, there grew great,
Founders of a mighty state:
There the Sacred Fire divine
Burned within a wondrous shrine
Which Her statue glorified
Throughout many kingdoms wide.
There those children wore the crown
To their children handed down
Many and many a golden age
Blotted now from history's page;
Till the last of all the line
Leagued him with the other nine
Great Atlantic kings whose hosts
Ravaged all the Mid Sea coasts:

Then the whelming deluge rolled
Over all those regions old;
Thrice three thousand years before
Solon questioned Egypt's lore *

* Plato: the *Timæus*, and the *Critias*.

A Voice From The Nile

I COME from mountains under other stars
Than those reflected in my waters here;
Athwart broad realms, beneath large skies, I flow,
Between the Libyan and Arabian hills,
And merge at last into the great Mid Sea;
And make this land of Egypt. All is mine:
The palm-trees and the doves among the palms,
The corn-fields and the flowers among the corn,
The patient oxen and the crocodiles,
The ibis and the heron and the hawk,
The lotus and the thick papyrus reeds,
The slant-sailed boats that flit before the wind
Or up my rapids ropes hale heavily;
Yea, even all the massive temple-fronts
With all their columns and huge effigies,
The pyramids and Memnon and the Sphinx,
This Cairo and the City of the Greek
As Memphis and the hundred-gated Thebes,
Sais and Denderah of Isis queen;
Have grown because I fed them with full life,
And flourish only while I feed them still,
For if I stint my fertilising flood,
Gaunt famine reaps among the sons of men
Who have not corn to reap for all they sowed,
And blight and languishment are everywhere;
And when I have withdrawn or turned aside
To other realms my ever-flowing streams,
The old realms withered from their old renown,
The sands came over them, the desert-sands
Incessantly encroaching, numberless
Beyond my water-drops, and buried them,

And all is silence, solitude, and death,
Exanimate silence while the waste winds howl
Over the sad immeasurable waste.

   Dusk memories haunt me of an infinite past,
Ages and cycles brood above my springs,
Though I remember not my primal birth.
So ancient is my being and august,
I know not anything more venerable;
Unless, perchance, the vaulting skies that hold
The sun and moon and stars that shine on me;
The air that breathes upon me with delight;
And Earth, All-Mother, all-beneficent,
Who held her mountains forth like opulent breasts
To cradle me and feed me with their snows,
And hollowed out the great sea to receive
My overplus of flowing energy:
Blessed for ever be our Mother Earth.

   Only, the mountains that must feed my springs
Year after year and every year with snows
As they have fed innumerable years,
These mountains they are evermore the same,
Rooted and motionless; the solemn heavens
Are evermore the same in stable rest;
The sun and moon and stars that shine on me
Are evermore the same although they move:
I solely, moving ever without pause,
Am evermore the same and not the same;
Pouring myself away into the sea,
And self-renewing from the farthest heights;
Ever-fresh waters streaming down and down,
The one old Nilus constant through their change.

The creatures also whom I breed and feed
Perpetually perish and dissolve,
And other creatures like them take their place,
To perish in their turn and be no more:
My profluent waters perish not from life,
Absorbed into the ever-living sea
Whose life is in their full replenishment.

Of all these creatures whom I breed and feed,
One only with his works is strange to me,
Is strange and admirable and pitiable,
As homeless where all others are at home.
My crocodiles are happy in my slime,
And bask and seize their prey, each for itselt,
And leave their eggs to hatch in the hot sun,
And die, their lives fulfilled, and are no more,
And others bask and prey and leave their eggs.
My doves they build their nests, each pair its own,
And feed their callow young, each pair its own,
None serves another, each one serves itself;
All glean alike about my fields of grain,
And all the nests they build them are alike,
And are the self-same nests they built of old
Before the rearing of the pyramids,
Before great Hekatompylos was reared;
Their cooing is the cooing soft and sweet
That murmured plaintively at evening-tide
In pillared Karnac as its pillars rose;
And they are happy floating through my palms.

But Man, the admirable, the pitiable,
These sad-eyed peoples of the sons of men,
Are as the children of an alien race
Planted among my children, not at home,

168

Changelings aloof from all my family.
The one is servant and the other lord,
And many myriads serve a single lord:
So was it when the pyramids were reared,
And sphinxes and huge columns and wrought stones
Were haled long lengthening leagues adown my banks
By hundreds groaning with the stress of toil,
And groaning under the taskmaster's scourge,
With many falling foredone by the way.
Half-starved on lentils, onions, and scant bread;
So is it now with these poor fellaheen
To whom my annual bounty brings fierce toil
With scarce enough of food to keep-in life.
They build mud huts and spacious palaces;
And in the huts the moiling millions dwell,
And in the palaces their sumptuous lords
Pampered with all the choicest things I yield:
Most admirable, most pitiable Man.

  Also their peoples ever are at war,
Slaying and slain, burning and ravaging,
And one yields to another and they pass,
While I flow evermore, the same great Nile,
The ever-young and ever-ancient Nile:
The swarthy is succeeded by the dusk,
The dusky by the pale, the pale again
By sunburned turbaned tribes long-linen-robed:
And with these changes all things change and pass,
All things but Me and this old Land of mine,
Their dwellings, habitudes, and garbs, and tongues:
I hear strange voices;* never more the voice
Austere priests chanted to the boat of death
Gliding across the Acherusian lake,
Or satraps parleyed in the Pharaoh's halls;

Never the voice of mad Cambyses' hosts,
Never the voice of Alexander's Greece,
Never the voice of Cæsar's haughty Rome:
And with the peoples and the languages,
With the great Empires still the great Creeds change;
They shift, they change, they vanish like thin dreams,
As unsubstantial as the mists that rise
After my overflow from out my fields,
In silver fleeces, golden volumes, rise,
And melt away before the mounting sun;
While I flow onward solely permanent
Amidst their swiftly-passing pageantry.

Poor men, most admirable, most pitiable,
With all their changes all their great Creeds change:
For Man, this alien in my family,
Is alien most in this, to cherish dreams
And brood on visions of eternity,
And build religions in his brooding brain
And in the dark depths awe-full of his soul.
My other children live their little lives,
Are born and reach their prime and slowly fail,
And all their little lives are self-fulfilled;
They die and are no more, content with age
And weary with infirmity. But Man
Has fear and hope and phantasy and awe,
And wistful yearnings and unsated loves,
That strain beyond the limits of his life,
And therefore Gods and Demons, Heaven and Hell:
This Man, the admirable, the pitiable.

Lo, I look backward some few thousand years,
And see men hewing temples in my rocks
With seated forms gigantic fronting them,

And solemn labyrinthine catacombs
With tombs all pictured with fair scenes of life
And scenes and symbols of mysterious death;
And planting avenues of sphinxes forth,
Sphinxes couched calm, whose passionless regard
Sets timeless riddles to bewildered time,
Forth from my sacred banks to other fanes
Islanded in the boundless sea of air,
Upon whose walls and colonnades are carved
Tremendous hieroglyphs of secret things;
I see embalming of the bodies dead
And judging of the disembodied souls;
I see the sacred animals alive,
And statues of the various-headed gods,
Among them throned a woman and a babe,
The goddess crescent-horned, the babe divine!
Then I flow forward some few thousand years,
And see new temples shining with all grace,
Whose sculptured gods are beautiful human forms.
Then I flow forward not a thousand years,
And see again a woman and a babe,
The woman haloed and the babe divine;
And everywhere that symbol of the cross
I knew aforetime in the ancient days,
The emblem then of life, but now of death.
Then I flow forward some few hundred years,
And see again the crescent, now supreme
On lofty cupolas and minarets
Whence voices sweet and solemn call to prayer.
So the men change along my changeless stream,
And change their faiths; but I yield all alike
Sweet water for their drinking, sweet as wine,
And pure sweet water for their lustral rites:
For thirty generations of my corn

Outlast a generation of my men,
And thirty generations of my men
Outlast a generation of their gods:
O admirable, pitiable Man,
My child yet alien in my family.

   And I through all these generations flow
Of corn and men and gods, all-bountiful,
Perennial through their transientness, still fed
By earth with waters in abundancy;
And as I flowed here long before they were,
So may I flow when they no longer are,
Most like the serpent of eternity:
Blessèd for ever be our Mother Earth.

* "and Nilus heareth strange voices." - *Sir Thomas Browne.*

The Lord Of The Castle Of Indolence

NOR did we lack our own right royal king,
  The glory of our peaceful realm and race.
By no long years of restless travailing,
  By no fierce wars or intrigues bland and base,
  Did he attain his superlofty place:
But one fair day he lounging to the throne
  Reclined thereon with such possessing grace
That all could see it was in sooth his own,
That it for him was fit and he for it alone.

He there reclined as lilies on a river,
  All cool in sunfire, float in buoyant rest;
He stirred as flowers that in the sweet south quiver;
  He moved as swans move on a lake's calm breast,
  Or clouds slow gliding in the golden west;
He thought as birds may think when 'mid the trees
  Their joy showers music o'er the brood-filled nest;
He swayed us all with ever placid ease
As sways the thronèd moon her world-wide wandering seas.

Look as within some fair and princely hall
  The marble statue of a god may rest,
Admired in silent reverence by all;
  Soothing the weary brain and anguished breast,
  By life's sore burthens all-too-much oppressed,
With visions of tranquillity supreme;
  So, self-sufficing, grand and bland and blest,
He dwelt enthroned, and whoso gazed did seem
Endowed with death-calm life in long unwistful dream.

While others fumed and schemed and toiled in vain
  To mould the world according to their mood,
He did by might of perfect faith refrain
  From any part in such disturbance rude.
  The world, he said, indeed is very good,
Its Maker surely wiser far than we;
  Feed soul and flesh upon its bounteous food,
Nor fret because of ill; All-good is He,
And worketh not in years but in Eternity.

How men will strain to row against the tide,
  Which yet must sweep them down in its career!
Or if some win their way and crown their pride,
  What do they win? the desert wild and drear,
  The savage rocks, the icy wastes austere,
Wherefrom the river's turbid rills downflow:
  But he upon the waters broad and clear,
In harmony with all the winds that blow,
'Mid cities, fields and farms, went drifting to and fro.

The king with constant heed must rule his realm,
  The soldier faint and starve in marches long,
The sailor guide with sleepless care his helm,
  The poet from sick languors soar in song:
  But he alone amidst the troubled throng
In restful ease diffused beneficence;
  Most like a mid-year noontide rich and strong,
That fills the earth with fruitful life intense,
And yet doth trance it all in sweetest indolence

When summer reigns the joyous leaves and flowers
  Steal imperceptibly upon the tree;
So stole upon him all his bounteous hours,
  So passive to their influence seemed he,

So clothed they him with joy and majesty;
Basking in ripest summer all his time,
  We blessed his shade and sang him songs of glee;
The dew and sunbeams fed his perfect prime,
And rooted broad and deep he broadly towered sublime.

Thus could he laugh those great and generous laughs
  Which made us love ourselves, the world, and him
And while they rang we felt as one who quaffs
  Some potent wine-cup dowered to the brim,
  And straightway all things seem to reel and swim,—
Suns, moons, earth, stars sweep through the vast profound,
  Wrapt in a golden mist-light warm and dim,
Rolled in a volume of triumphant sound;
So in that laughter's joy the whole world carolled round.

The sea, the sky, wood, mountain, stream and plain,
  Our whole fair world did serve him and adorn,
Most like some casual robe which he might deign
  To use when kinglier vesture was not worn.
  Was all its being by his soul upborne,
That it should render homage so complete?
  The day and night, the even and the morn,
Seemed ever circling grateful round his feet,
'With Thee, through Thee we live this rich life pure and sweet!'

For while he loved our broad world beautiful,
  His placid wisdom penetrated it,
And found the lovely words but poor and dull
  Beside the secret splendours they transmit,
  The heavenly things in earthly symbols writ:
He knew the blood-red sweetness of the vine,
  Yet did not therefore at the revel sit;
But straining out the very wine of wine,
Lived calm and pure and glad in drunkenness divine.

Without an effort the imperial sun
  With ever ample life of light doth feed
The spheres revolving round it every one:
  So all his heart and soul and thought and deed
  Flowed freely forth for every brother's need;
He knew no difference between good and ill,
  But as the sun doth nourish flower and weed
With self-same bounty, he too ever still
Lived blessing all alike with equal loving will.

The all-bestowing sun is clothed with splendour,
  The all-supporting sun doth reign supreme;
So must eternal justice ever render
  Each unsought payment to its last extreme:
  Thus he most rich in others' joy did seem,
And reigned by servitude all-effortless;
  For heaven and earth must vanish like a dream
Ere such a soul divine can know distress,
Whom all the laws of Life conspire to love and bless.

The Poet And His Muse

I SIGHED unto my Muse, "O gentle Muse,
  Would you but come and kiss my aching brow,
And thus a little life and joy infuse
  Into my brain and heart so weary now;
Into my heart so sad with emptiness
Even when unafflicted by the stress
    Of all our kind's poor life;
Into my brain so feeble and so listless,
Crushed down by burthens of dark thought resistless
Of all our want and woe and unresulting strife.

"Would you but come and kiss me on the brow,
  Would you but kiss me on the pallid lips
That have so many years been songless now,
  And on the eyes involved in drear eclipse;
That thus the barren brain long overwrought
Might yield again some blossoms of glad thought,
    And the long-mute lips sing,
And the long-arid eyes grow moist and tender
With some new vision of the ancient splendour
Of beauty and delight that lives in everything.

"Would you but kiss me on the silent lips
  And teach them thus to sing some new sweet song;
Would you but kiss my eyes from their eclipse
  With some new tale of old-world right and wrong:
Some song of love and joy or tender grief
Whose sweetness is its own divine relief,
    Whose joy is golden bliss;
Some solemn and impassioned antique story
Where love against dark doom burns out in glory,
Where life is freely staked to win one mutual kiss.

"Would you but sing to me some new dear song
  Of love in bliss or bale alike supreme;
Some story of our old-world right and wrong
  With noble passion burning through the theme:
What though the story be of darkest doom,
If loyal spirits shining through its gloom
      Throb to us from afar?
What though the song with heavy sorrows languish,
If loving hearts pulse to us through its anguish?
Is not the whole black night enriched by one pure star?"

And lo! She came, the ever-gentle Muse,
  Sad as my heart, and languid as my brain;
Too gentle in her loving to refuse,
  Although her steps were weariness and pain;
Although her eyes were blank and lustreless,
Although her form was clothed with heaviness
      And drooped beneath the weight;
Although her lips were blanched from all their
      blooming,
Her pure face pallid as from long entombing,
Her bright regard and smile sombre and desolate.—

"Sad as thy heart and languid as thy brain
  I come unto thy sighing through the gloom,
I come with mortal weariness and pain,
  I come as one compelled to leave her tomb:
Behold, am I not wrapt as in the cloud
Of death's investiture and sombre shroud?
      Am I not wan as death!
Look at the withered leafage of my garland,
Is it not nightshade from the sad dim far land
Of night and old oblivion and no mortal breath?

"I come unto thy sighing through the gloom,
  My hair dishevelled dank with dews of night,
Reluctantly constrained to leave my tomb;
  With eyes that have for ever lost their light;
My vesture mouldering with deep death's disgrace,
My heart as chill and bloodless as my face,
    My forehead like a stone;
My spirit sightless as my eyes are sightless,
My inmost being nerveless, soulless, lightless,
My joyous singing voice a harsh sepulchral moan.

"My hair dishevelled dank with dews of night,
  From that far region of dim death I come,
With eyes and soul and spirit void of light,
  With lips more sad in speech than stark and dumb:
Lo, you have ravaged me with dolorous thought
Until my brain was wholly overwrought,
    Barren of flowers and fruit;
Until my heart was bloodless for all passion,
Until my trembling lips could no more fashion
Sweet words to fit sweet airs of trembling lyre and lute.

"From the sad regions of dim death I come;
  We tell no tales there for our tale is told,
We sing no songs there for our lips are dumb,
  Likewise our hearts and brains are graveyard mould;
No wreaths of laurel, myrtle, ivy or vine,
About our pale and pulseless brows entwine,
    And that sad frustrate realm
Nor amaranths nor asphodels can nourish,
But aconite and black-red poppies flourish
On such Lethean dews as fair life overwhelm.

"We tell no tales more, we whose tale is told;
  As your brain withered and your heart grew chill
My heart and brain were turned to churchyard mould,
  Wherefore my singing voice sank ever still:
And I, all heart and brain and voice, am dead;
It is my Phantom here beside your bed
     That speaketh to you now;
Though you exist still, a mere form inurning
The ashes of dead fires of thought and yearning,
Dead faith, dead love, dead hope, in hollow breast and
     brow."

When it had moaned these words of hopeless doom,
  The Phantom of the Muse once young and fair,
Pallid and dim from its disastrous tomb,
  Of Her so sweet and young and *débonnaire*,
So rich of heart and brain and singing voice,
So quick to shed sweet tears and to rejoice
     And smile with ravishing grace;
My soul was stupefied by its own reaping,
Then burst into a flood of passionate weeping,
Tears bitter as black blood streaming adown my face.

"O Muse, so young and sweet and glad and fair,
  O Muse of hope and faith and joy and love,
O Muse so gracious and so *débonnaire*,
  Darling of earth beneath and heaven above;
If Thou art gone into oblivious death,
Why should I still prolong my painful breath?
     Why still exist, the urn
Holding of once-great fires the long dead ashes,
No sole spark left of all their glow and flashes,
Fires never to rekindle more and shine and burn?

"O Muse of hope and faith and joy and love,
  Soul of my soul, if Thou in truth art dead,
A mournful alien in our world above,
  A Phantom moaning by my midnight bed;
How can I be alive, a hollow form
With ashes of dead fires once bright and warm?
    What thing is worth my strife?
The Past a great regret, the Present sterile,
The Future hopeless, with the further peril
Of withering down and down to utter death-in-life.

"Soul of my soul, canst Thou indeed be dead?
  What mean for me if I accept their lore,
Thy words, O Phantom moaning by my bed,
  "I cannot sing again for evermore"?
I nevermore can think or feel or dream
Or hope or love—the fatal loss supreme!
    I am a soulless clod;
No germ of life within me that surpasses
The little germs of weeds and flowers and grasses
Wherewith our liberal Mother decks the graveyard sod.

"I am half-torpid yet I spurn this lore,
  I am long silent yet cannot avow
My singing voice is lost for evermore;
  For lo, this beating heart, this burning brow,
This spirit gasping in keen spasms of dread
And fierce revulsion that it is not dead,
    This agony of the sting:
What soulless clod could have these tears and sobbings,
These terrors that are hopes, these passionate, throbbings?
Dear Muse, revive! we yet may dream and love and sing!"

Mater Tenebrarum

IN the endless nights, from my bed, where sleepless in anguish
    I lie,
I startle the stillness and gloom with a bitter and strong cry:
O Love! O Belovèd long lost! come down from thy Heaven above,
For my heart is wasting and dying in uttermost famine for love!
Come down for a moment! oh, come! Come serious and mild
And pale, as thou wert on this earth, thou adorable Child!
Or come as thou art, with thy sanctitude, triumph and bliss,
For a garment of glory about thee; and give me one kiss,
One tender and pitying look of thy tenderest eyes,
One word of solemn assurance and truth that the soul with its
    love never dies!

In the endless nights, from my bed, where sleepless in frenzy I lie,
I cleave through the crushing gloom with a bitter and deadly cry:
Oh! where have they taken my Love from our Eden of bliss on
    this earth,
Which now is a frozen waste of sepulchral and horrible dearth?
Have they killed her indeed? is her soul as her body, which long
Has mouldered away in the dust where the foul worms throng?
O'er what abhorrent Lethes, to what remotest star,
Is she rapt away from my pursuit through cycles and systems far?
She is dead, she is utterly dead; for her life would hear and speed
To the wild imploring cry of my heart that cries in its dreadful need.

In the endless nights, on my bed, where sleeplessly brooding I lie,
I burden the heavy gloom with a bitter and weary sigh:
No hope in this worn-out world, no hope beyond the tomb;
No living and loving God, but blind and stony Doom.
Anguish and grief and sin, terror, disease and despair:
Why throw not off this life, this garment of torture I wear,

And go down to sleep in the grave in everlasting rest?
What keeps me yet in this life, what spark in my frozen breast?
A fire of dread, a light of hope, kindled, O Love, by thee;
For thy pure and gentle and beautiful soul, it must immortal be.

The Three That Shall Be One

LOVE on the earth alit,
Come to be Lord of it;
Looked round and laughed with glee,
Noble my empery!
Straight ere that laugh was done
Sprang forth the royal sun,
Pouring out golden shine
Over the realm divine.

Came then a lovely may,
Dazzling the new-born day,
Wreathing her golden hair
With the red roses there,
Laughing with sunny eyes
Up to the sunny skies,
Moving so light and free
To her own minstrelsy.

Love with swift rapture cried,
Dear Life, thou art my bride!
Whereto, with fearless pride,
Dear Love, indeed thy bride!
All the earth's fruit and flowers,
All the world's wealth are ours;
Sun, moon, and stars gem
Our marriage diadem.

So they together fare,
Lovely and joyous pair;
So hand in hand they roam
All through their Eden home;

Each to the other's sight
An ever-new delight:
Blue heaven and blooming earth
Joy in their darling's mirth.

Who comes to meet them now,—
She with the pallid brow,
Wreathing her night-dark hair
With the red poppies there,
Pouring from solemn eyes
Gloom through the sunny skies,
Moving so silently
In her deep reverie?

Life paled as she drew near,
Love shook with doubt and fear.
Ah, then, she said, in truth
(Eyes full of yearning ruth),
Love, thou would'st have this Life,
Fair may! to be thy wife?
Yet at an awful shrine
Wert thou not plighted mine?

Pale, paler poor Life grew;
Love murmured, It is true!
How could I thee forsake?
From the brief dream I wake.
Yet, O belovèd Death,
See how *she* suffereth;
Ere we from earth depart
Soothe her, thou tender heart!

Faint on the ground she lay;
Love kissed the swoon away;

Death then bent over her,
Death the sweet comforter!
Whispered with tearful smile,
Wait but a little while,
Then I will come for thee;
We are one family.

A Polish Insurgent

WHAT would you have? said I;*
'Tis so easy to go and die,
'Tis so hard to stay and live,
In this alien peace and this comfort callous,
Where only the murderers get the gallows,
Where the jails are for rogues who thieve.

'Tis so easy to go and die,
Where our Country, our Mother, the Martyr,
Moaning in bonds doth lie,
Bleeding with stabs in her breast,
Her throat with a foul clutch prest,
Under the thrice-accursed Tartar.

But Smith, your man of sense,
Ruddy, and broad, and round—like so!
Kindly— but dense, but dense,
Said to me: 'Do not go:
It is hopeless; right is wrong;
The tyrant is too strong.'

Must a man have *hope* to fight?
Can a man not fight in despair?
Must the soul cower down for the body's weakness,
And slaver the devil's hoof with meekness,
Nor care nor dare to share
Certain defeat with the right?

They do not know us, my Mother!
They know not our love, our hate!
And how we would die with each other,

Embracing proud and elate,
Rather than live apart
In peace with shame in the heart.

No hope!—If a heavy anger
Our God hath treasured against us long,
His lightning-shafts from His thunder-clangour
Raining a century down:
We have loved when we went most wrong;
He cannot for ever frown.

No hope!—We can haste to be killed,
That the tale of the victims get filled;
The more of the debt we pay,
The less on our sons shall weigh:
This star through the baleful rack of the cope
Burns red; red is our hope.

O our Mother, thou art noble and fair!
Fair and proud and chaste, thou Queen!
Chained and stabbed in the breast,
Thy throat with a foul clutch prest;
Yet around thee how coarse, how mean,
Are these rich shopwives who stare!

Art thou moaning, O our Mother, through the swoon
Of thine agony of desolation?
'Do my sons still love me? or can they stand
Gazing afar from a foreign land,
Loving more peace and gold—the boon
Of a people strange, of a sordid nation?'

O our Mother, moan not thus!
We love you as you love us,

And our hearts are wild with thy sorrow:
If we cannot save thee, we are blest
Who can die on thy sacred bleeding breast.—
    So we left Smith-Land on the morrow,
    And we hasten across the West.

* Some time after writing this I found that the great BALZAC, in *La Cousine Bette,* dwells
on this very phrase, 'Que voulez-vous?' as characteristic of the gallant and reckless Poles.

The Sleeper

THE fire is in a steadfast glow,
  The curtains drawn against the night;
Upon the red couch soft and low
  Between the fire and lamp alight
She rests half-sitting, half-reclining
Encompassed by the cosy shining,
  Her ruby dress with lace trimmed white.

Her left hand shades her drooping eyes
  Against the fervour of the fire,
The right upon her cincture lies
  In languid grace beyond desire,
A lily fallen among roses;
So placidly her form reposes,
  It scarcely seemeth to respire.

She is not surely all awake,
  As yet she is not all asleep;
The eyes with lids half-open take
  A startled deprecating peep
Of quivering drowsiness, then slowly
The lids sink back, before she wholly
  Resigns herself to slumber deep.

The side-neck gleams so pure beneath
  The underfringe of gossamer,
The tendrils of whose faery wreath
  The softest sigh suppressed would stir.
The little pink-shell ear-rim flushes
With her young blood's translucent blushes,
  Nestling in tresses warm as fur.

The contour of her cheek and chin
  Is curved in one delicious line,
Pure as a vase of porcelain thin
  Through which a tender light may shine;
Her brow and blue-veined temple gleaming
Beneath the dusk of hair back-streaming
  Are as a virgin's marble shrine.

The ear is burning crimson fire,
  The flush is brightening on the face,
The lips are parting to suspire,
  The hair grows restless in its place
As if itself new tangles wreathing;
The bosom with her deeper breathing
  Swells and subsides with ravishing grace.

The hand slides softly to caress,
  Unconscious, that fine-pencilled curve
'Her lip's contour and downiness,'
  Unbending with a sweet reserve;
A tender darkness that abashes
Steals out beneath the long dark lashes,
  Whose sightless eyes make eyesight swerve.

The hand on chin and throat downslips,
  Then softly, softly on her breast;
A dream comes fluttering o'er the lips,
  And stirs the eyelids in their rest,
And makes their undershadows quiver,
And like a ripple on a river
  Glides through her breathing manifest

I feel an awe to read this dream
  So clearly written in her smile;

A pleasant not a passionate theme,
  A little love, a little guile;
I fear lest she should speak revealing
The secret of some maiden feeling
  I have no right to hear the while.

The dream has passed without a word
  Of all that hovered finely traced;
The hand has slipt down, gently stirred
  To join the other at her waist;
Her breath from that light agitation
Has settled to its slow pulsation;
  She is by deep sleep re-embraced.

Deep sleep, so holy in its calm,
  So helpless, yet so awful too;
Whose silence sheds as sweet a balm
  As ever sweetest voice could do;
Whose trancèd eyes, unseen, unseeing
Shadowed by pure love, thrill our being
  With tender yearnings through and through.

Sweet sleep; no hope, no fear, no strife;
  The solemn sanctity of death,
With all the loveliest bloom of life;
  Eternal peace in mortal breath:
Pure sleep from which she will awaken
Refreshed as one who hath partaken
  New strength, new hope, new love, new faith.

At Belvoir

Sunday, July 3, 1881.

A BALLAD, HISTORICAL AND PROPHETIC.

'In maiden meditation, fancy free.'

MY thoughts go back to last July,
   Sweet happy thoughts and tender;—
'The bridal of the earth and sky,'
   A day of noble splendour;
A day to make the saddest heart
   In joy a true believer;
When two good friends we roamed apart
   The shady walks of Belvoir.

A maiden like a budding rose,
   Unconscious of the golden
And fragrant bliss of love that glows
   Deep in her heart infolden;
A Poet old in years and thought,
   Yet not too old for pleasance,
Made young again and fancy-fraught
   By such a sweet friend's presence.

The other two beyond our ken
   Most shamefully deserted,
And far from all the ways of men
   Their stealthy steps averted:
Of course our Jack would go astray,
   Erotic and erratic;
But Mary! —well, I own the day
   Was really too ecstatic.

We roamed with many a merry jest
    And many a ringing laughter;
The slow calm hours too rich in zest
    To heed before and after:
Yet lingering down the lovely walks
    Soft strains anon came stealing,
A finer music through our talks
    Of sweeter, deeper feeling:

Yes, now and then a quiet word
    Of seriousness dissembling
In smiles would touch some hidden chord
    And set it all a-trembling:
I trembled too, and felt it strange;—
    Could I be in possession
Of music richer in its range
    Than yet had found expression?

The cattle standing in the mere,
    The swans upon it gliding,
The sunlight on the waters clear,
    The radiant clouds dividing;
The solemn sapphire sky above,
    The foliage lightly waving,
The soft air's Sabbath peace and love
    To satisfy all craving.

We mapped the whole fair region out
    As Country of the Tender,
From first pursuit in fear and doubt
    To final glad surrender:
Each knoll and arbour got its name,
    Each vista, covert, dingle;—

No young pair now may track the same
    And long continue single!

And in the spot most thrilling-sweet
    Of all this Love-Realm rosy
Our truant pair had found retreat,
    Unblushing, calm and cosy:
Where seats too wide for one are placed,
    And yet for two but narrow,
It's 'Let my arm steal round your waist,
    And be my winsome marrow!'

Reclining on a pleasant lea
    Such tender scenes rehearsing,
A freakish fit seized him and me
    For wildly foolish versing:
We versed of this, we versed of that,
    A pair of mocking sinners,
While our lost couple strayed or sat
    Oblivious of their dinners.

But what was strange, our maddest rhymes
    In all their divagations
Were charged and over-charged at times
    With deep vaticinations:
I yearn with wonder at the power
    Of Poetry prophetic
Which in my soul made that blithe hour
    With this hour sympathetic.

For though we are in winter now,
    My heart is in full summer:
Old Year, old Wish, have made their bow;
    I welcome each new-comer.

'The King is dead, long live the King
    The throne is vacant never!'
Is true, I read, of everything,
    So of my heart for ever!

My thoughts go on to next July,
    More happy thoughts, more tender;
'The bridal of the earth and sky,'
    A day of perfect splendour;
A day to make the saddest heart
    In bliss a firm believer;
When two True Loves may roam apart
    The shadiest walks of Belvoir.

There may be less of merry jest
    And less of ringing laughter,
Yet life be much more rich in zest
    And richer still thereafter;
The love-scenes of that region fair
    Have very real rehearsing,
And tremulous kisses thrill the air
    Far sweetlier than sweet versing;

The bud full blown at length reveal
    Its deepest golden burning;
The heart inspired with love unseal
    Its inmost passionate yearning:
The music of the hidden chord
    At length find full expression;
The Seraph of the Flaming Sword
    Assume divine possession.

Polycrates On Waterloo Bridge

LET no mortals dare to be
Happier in their lives than we:
Thus the jealous gods decree.

This decree was never heard,
Never by their lips averred,
Yet on high stands registered.

I have read it, and I fear
All the gods above, my Dear,
All must envy us two here.

Let us, then, propitiate
These proud satraps of sole Fate;
Our hearts' wealth is all too great

Say, what rich and cherished thing
Can I to the river fling
As a solemn offering?

O belovèd Meerschaum Pipe,
Whose pink bloom would soon be ripe,
Must thou be the chosen type?

Cloud-compeller! Foam o' the Sea,
Whence rose Venus fair and free
On some poet's reverie!

In the sumptuous silken-lined
Case where thou hast lain enshrined
Thou must now a coffin find!

And, to drag thee surely down,
Lo! I tie my last half-crown:
We shall have to walk through town.

Penny toll is paid, and thus
All the bridge is free to us;
But no cab, nor even a 'bus!

Far I fling thee through the gloom;
Sink into the watery tomb,
O thou consecrate to Doom!

May no sharp police, while they track
Spoils thrown after some great 'crack,'
Ever, ever bring thee back!

No mudlarkers, who explore
Every ebb the filthy floor,
Bring thee to the day once more!

No sleek cook—I spare the wish;
Dead dogs, cats, and suchlike fish,
Surely are not yet a dish? . . .

Gods! the dearest, as I wis,
Of my treasures offered is;
Pardon us our heavenly bliss!

What Voice murmurs full of spleen?
Not that Pipe, but— Ssss! how mean
All the gods have ever been!

Day

WAKING one morning
In a pleasant land,
By a river flowing
Over golden sand:—

Whence flow ye, waters,
O'er your golden sand?
We come flowing
From the Silent Land.

Whither flow ye, waters,
O'er your golden sand?
We go flowing
To the Silent Land.

And what is this fair realm?
A grain of golden sand
In the great darkness
Of the Silent Land.

Night

HE cried out through the night:
    'Where is the light?
    Shall nevermore
    Open Heaven's door?
    Oh, I am left
    Lonely, bereft!'

He cried out through the night:
    It spread vaguely white,
    With its ghost of a moon
    Above the dark swoon
    Of the earth lying chill,
    Breathless, grave still.

He cried out through the night:
    His voice in its might
    Rang forth far and far,
    And then like a star
    Dwindled from sense
    In the Immense.

He cried out through the night:
    No answering light,
    No syllabled sound;
    Beneath and around
    A long shuddering thrill
    Then all again still.

Art

I

WHAT precious things are you making fast
  In all these silken lines?
And where and to whom will it go at last?
  Such subtle knots and twines!

I am tying up all my love in this,
  With all its hopes and fears,
With all its anguish and all its bliss,
  And its hours as heavy as years.

I am going to send it afar, afar,
  To know not where above;
To that sphere beyond the highest star
  Where dwells the soul of my Love.

But in vain, in vain, would I make it fast
  With countless subtle twines;
For ever its fire breaks out at last,
  And shrivels all the lines.

II

If you have a carrier-dove
  That can fly over land and sea;
And a message for your Love,
  'Lady, I love but thee!'

And this dove will never stir
  But straight from her to you,

And straight from you to her,
  As you know and she knows too.

Will you first ensure, O sage,
  Your dove that never tires
With your message in a cage,
  Though a cage of golden wires?

Or will you fling your dove:
  'Fly, darling, without rest,
Over land and sea to my Love,
  And fold your wings in her breast'?

III

Singing is sweet; but be sure of this,
Lips only sing when they cannot kiss.

Did he ever suspire a tender lay
While her presence took his breath away?

Had his fingers been able to toy with her hair
Would they then have written the verses fair?

Had she let his arm steal round her waist
Would the lovely portrait yet be traced?

Since he could not embrace it flushed and warm,
He has carved in stone the perfect form.

Who gives the fine report of the feast?
He who got none and enjoyed it least.

Were the wine really slipping down his throat

Would his song of the wine advance a note?

Will you puff out the music that sways the whirl,
Or dance and make love with a pretty girl?

Who shall the great battle-story write?
Not the hero down in the thick of the fight.

Statues and pictures and verse may be grand,
But they are not the Life for which they stand.

Philosophy

I

HIS eyes found nothing beautiful and bright,
Nor wealth nor honour, glory nor delight,
Which he could grasp and keep with might and right

Flowers bloomed for maidens, swords outflashed for boys,
The world's big children had their various toys;
He could not feel their sorrows and their joys.

Hills held a secret they would not unfold,
In careless scorn of him the ocean rolled,
The stars were alien splendours high and cold.

He felt himself a king bereft of crown,
Defrauded from his birthright of renown,
Bred up in littleness with churl and clown.

II

How could he vindicate himself? His eyes,
That found not anywhere their proper prize,
Looked through and through the specious earth and skies.

They probed, and all things yielded to their probe;
They saw the void around the massy globe,
The raging fire within its flowery robe.

They pierced through beauty; saw the bones, the mesh
Of nerves and veins, the hideous raw red flesh,
Beneath the skin most delicate and fresh:

Saw Space a mist unfurled around the steep
Where plunge Time's waters to the blackest deep;
Saw Life a dream in Death's eternal sleep.

III

A certain fair form came before his sight,
Responding to him as the day to night:
To yearning, love; to cold and gloom, warm light.

A hope sprang from his breast, and fluttered far
On rainbow wings; beyond the cloudy bar,
Though very much beneath the nearest star.

His eyes drew back their beams to kindle fire
In his own heart; whose masterful desire
Scorned all beyond its aim, lower or higher.

This fire flung lustre upon grace and bloom,
Gave warmth and brightness to a little room,
Burned Thought to ashes in its fight with gloom.

IV

He said: Those eyes alone see well that view
Life's lovely surfaces of form and hue;
And not Death's entrails, looking through and through.

Bones, nerves and veins, and flesh are covered in
By this opaque transparency of skin,
Precisely that we should not see within.

The corpse is hid, that Death may work its vile

Corruption in black secrecy; the while
Our saddest graves with grass and fair flowers smile.

If you will analyse the bread you eat,
The water and the wine most pure and sweet,
Your stomach soon must loathe all drink and meat.

Life liveth but in Life, and doth not roam
To other realms if all be well at home:
'Solid as ocean-foam,' quoth ocean-foam.

If Midge will pine and curse its hours away
Because Midge is not Everything For-aye,
Poor Midge thus loses its one summer day;
Loses its all and winneth what, I pray?

Life's Hebe

IN the early morning-shine
Of a certain day divine,
I beheld a Maiden stand
With a pitcher in her hand;
Whence she poured into a cup
Until it was half filled up
Nectar that was golden light
In the cup of crystal bright.

And the first who took the cup
With pure water filled it up;
As he drank then, it was more
Ruddy golden than before;
And he leapt and danced and sang
As to Bacchic cymbals' clang.

But the next who took the cup
With the red wine filled it up;
What he drank then was in hue
Of a heavy sombre blue:
First he reeled and then he crept,
Then lay faint but never slept.

And the next who took the cup
With the white milk filled it up;
What he drank at first seemed blood,
Then turned thick and brown as rnud:
And he moved away as slow
As a weary ox may go.

But the next who took the cup
With sweet honey filled it up;
Nathless that which he did drink
Was thin fluid black as ink:
As he went he stumbled soon,
And lay still in deathlike swoon.

She the while without a word
Unto all the cup preferred:
Blandly smiled and sweetly laughed
As each mingled his own draught.

And the next who took the cup
To the sunshine held it up,
Gave it back and did not taste;
It was empty when replaced:
First he bowed a reverent bow,
Then he kissed her on the brow.

But the next who took the cup
Without mixture drank it up;
When she took it back from him
It was full unto the brim:
He with a right bold embrace
Kissed her sweet lips face to face.

Then she sang with blithest cheer:
Who has thirst, come here, come here!
Nectar that is golden light
In the cup of crystal bright,
Nectar that is sunny fire
Warm as warmest heart's desire:
Pitcher never lacketh more,
Arm is never tired to pour:

Honey, water, milk or wine
Mingle with the draught divine,
Drink it pure, or drink it not;
Each is free to choose his lot:
Am I old? or am I cold?
Only two have kissed me bold!

She was young and fair and gay
As that young and glorious day.

William Blake

HE came to the desert of London town
  Grey miles long;
He wandered up and he wandered down,
  Singing a quiet song.

He came to the desert of London town,
  Mirk miles broad;
He wandered up and he wandered down,
  Ever alone with God.

There were thousands and thousands of human kind
  In this desert of brick and stone:
But some were deaf and some were blind,
  And he was there alone.

At length the good hour came; he died
  As he had lived, alone:
He was not missed from the desert wide,
  Perhaps he was found at the Throne.

Robert Burns

HE felt scant need
Of church or creed,
He took small share
In saintly prayer,
His eyes found food for his love;
He could pity poor devils condemned to hell,
But sadly neglected endeavours to dwell
With the angels in luck above:
To save one's precious peculiar soul
He never could understand is the whole
Of a mortal's business in life,
While all about him his human kin
With loving and hating and virtue and sin
Reel overmatched in the strife.
'The heavens for the heavens, and the earth for the
earth!
I am a Man— I'll be true to my birth—
Man in my joys, in my pains.'
So fearless, stalwart, erect and free,
He gave to his fellows right royally
His strength, his heart, his brains;
For proud and fiery and swift and bold—
Wine of life from heart of gold,
The blood of his heathen manhood rolled
Full-billowed through his veins.

The Fire That Filled My Heart of Old

I

THE fire that filled my heart of old
  Gave lustre while it burned;
Now only ashes grey and cold
  Are in its silence urned.
Ah! better was the furious flame,
  The splendour with the smart:
I never cared for the singer's fame,
  But, oh! for the singer's heart
      Once more—
The burning fulgent heart!

II

No love, no hate, no hope, no fear,
  No anguish and no mirth;
Thus life extends from year to year,
  A flat of sullen dearth.
Ah! life's blood creepeth cold and tame,
  Life's thought plays no new part:
I never cared for the singer's fame,
  But oh! for the singer's heart
      Once more—
The bleeding passionate heart

Song

'THE Nightingale was not yet heard,
  For the Rose was not yet blown.'*
His heart was quiet as a bird
  Asleep in the night alone,
And never were its pulses stirred
  To breathe or joy or moan:
The Nightingale was not yet heard
  For the Rose was not yet blown.

Then She bloomed forth before his sight
  In passion and in power,
And filled the very day with light,
  So glorious was her dower;
And made the whole vast moonlit night
  As fragrant as a bower:
The young, the beautiful, the bright,
  The splendid peerless Flower.

Whereon his heart was like a bird
  When Summer mounts his throne,
And all its pulses thrilled and stirred
  To songs of joy and moan,
To every most impassioned word
  And most impassioned tone;
The Nightingale at length was heard
  For the Rose at length was blown.

* 'Traveller in Persia' (Mr. Binning); cited by Mr. Fitzgerald
in the notes to his translation of Omar Khayyam.

A Requiem

THOU hast lived in pain and woe,
A Thou hast lived in grief and fear;
Now thine heart can dread no blow,
Now thine eyes can shed no tear:
  Storms round us shall beat and rave;
  Thou art sheltered in the grave.

Thou for long, long years hast borne,
Bleeding through Life's wilderness,
Heavy loss and wounding scorn;
Now thine heart is burdenless:
  Vainly rest for ours we crave;
  Thine is quiet in the grave.

We must toil with pain and care,
We must front tremendous Fate,
We must fight with dark Despair;
Thou dost dwell in solemn state,
  Couched triumphant, calm and brave,
  In the ever-holy grave.

A Song Of Sighing

I

WOULD some little joy to-day
    Visit us, heart!
Could it but a moment stay,
    Then depart,
With the flutter of its wings
Stirring sense of brighter things.

II

Like a butterfly astray
    In a dark room;
Telling:—Outside there is day,
    Sweet flowers bloom,
Birds are singing, trees are green
Runnels ripple silver sheen.

III

Heart! we now have been so long
    Sad without change,
Shut in deep from shine and song
    Nor can range;
It would do us good to know
That the world is not all woe.

IV

Would some little joy to-day
    Visit us, heart!
Could it but a moment stay,
    Then depart,
With the lustre of its wings
Lighting dreams of happy things,
    O sad my heart!

Printed in the United States
142109LV00007B/74/P